I0406462

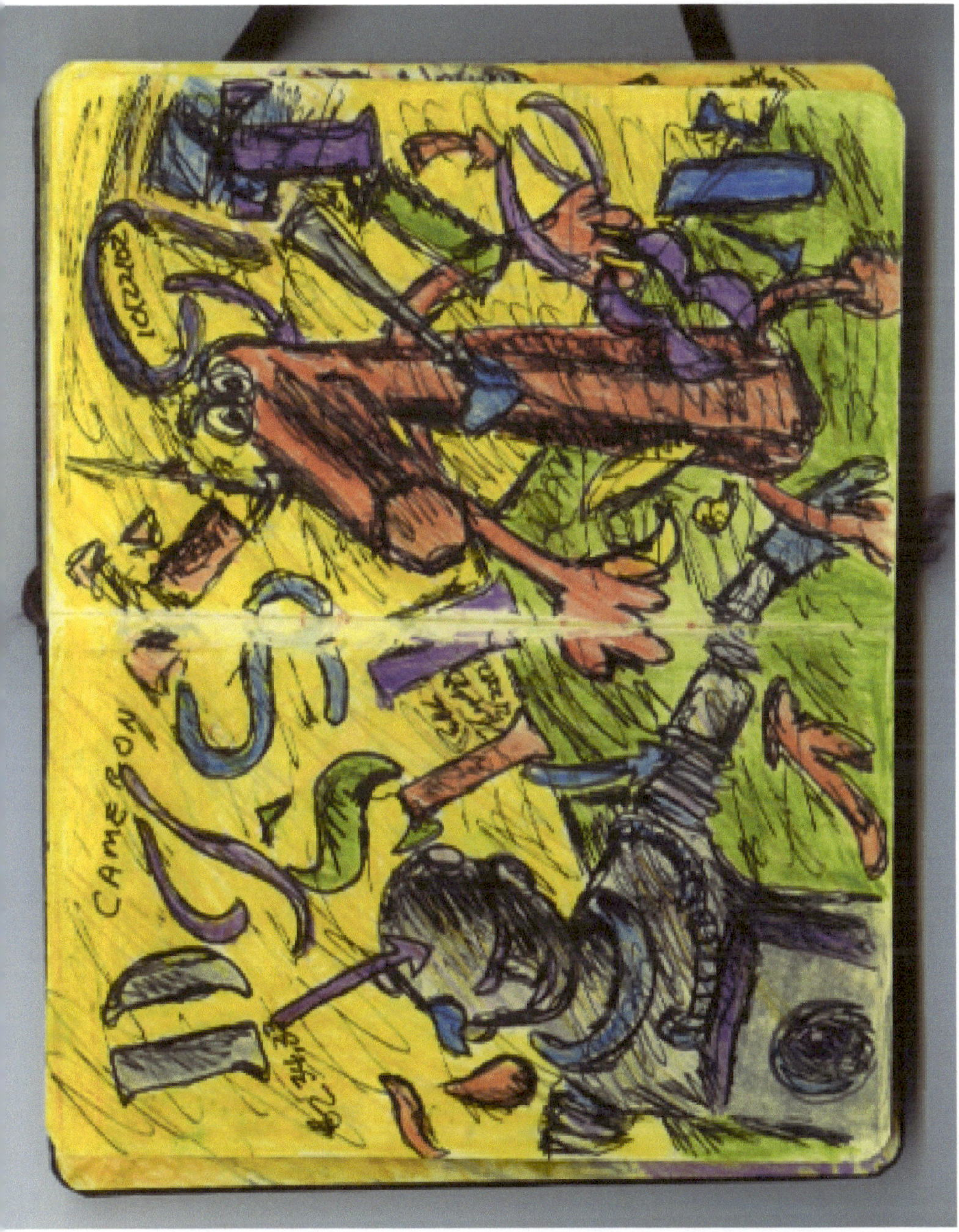

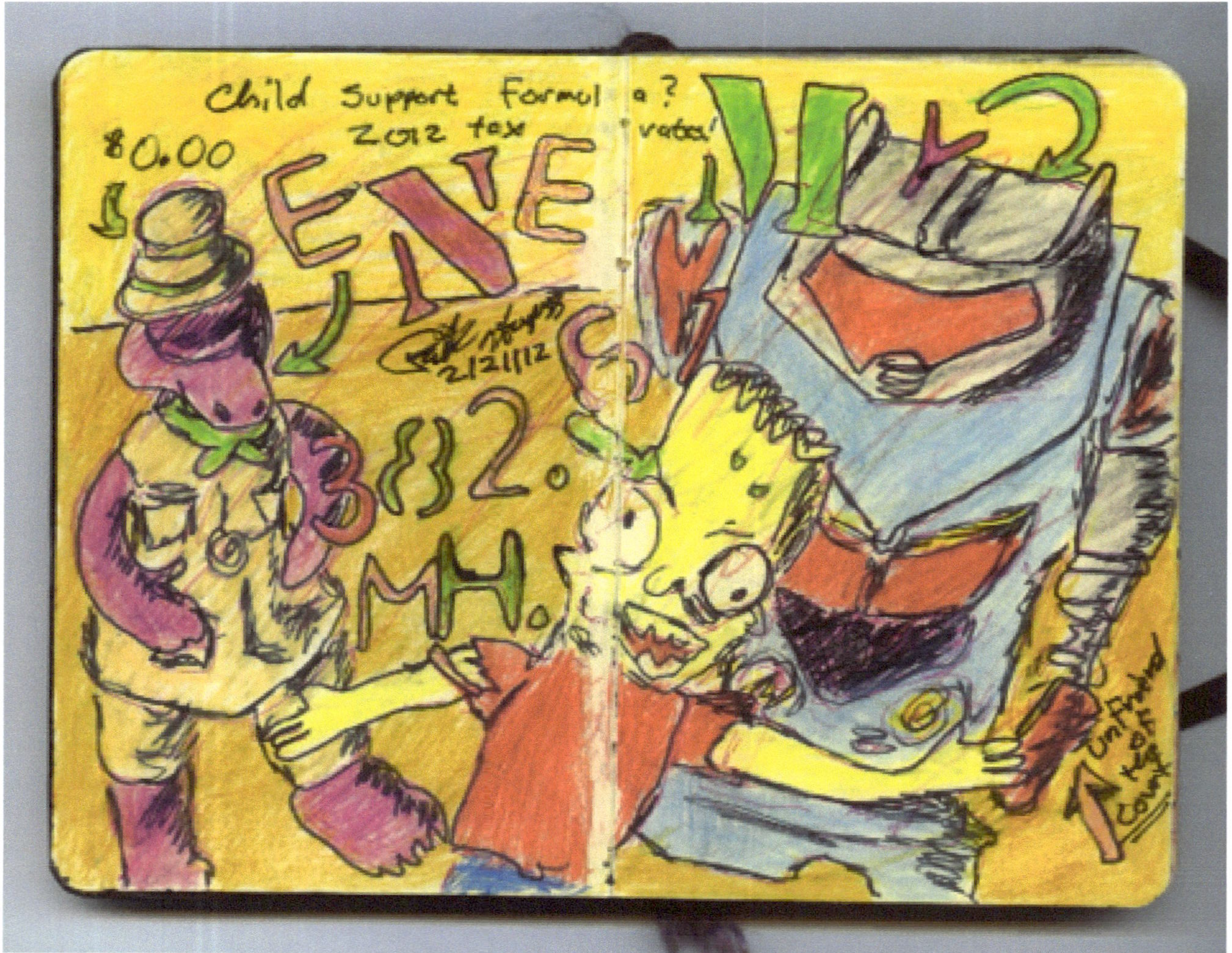
Child Support Formula?
2012 tax
data!
$0.00
Unfriended
to Count
2/21/12

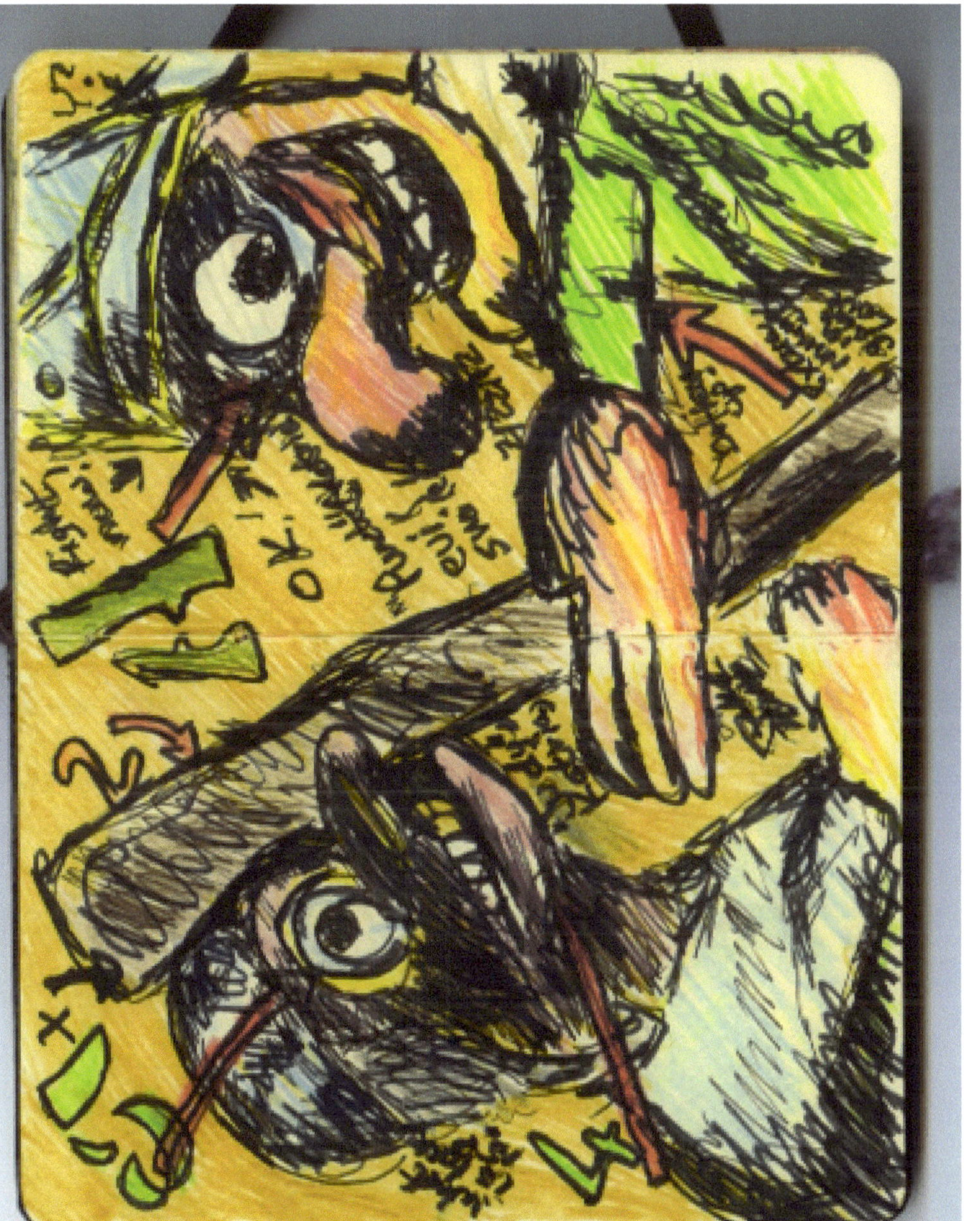

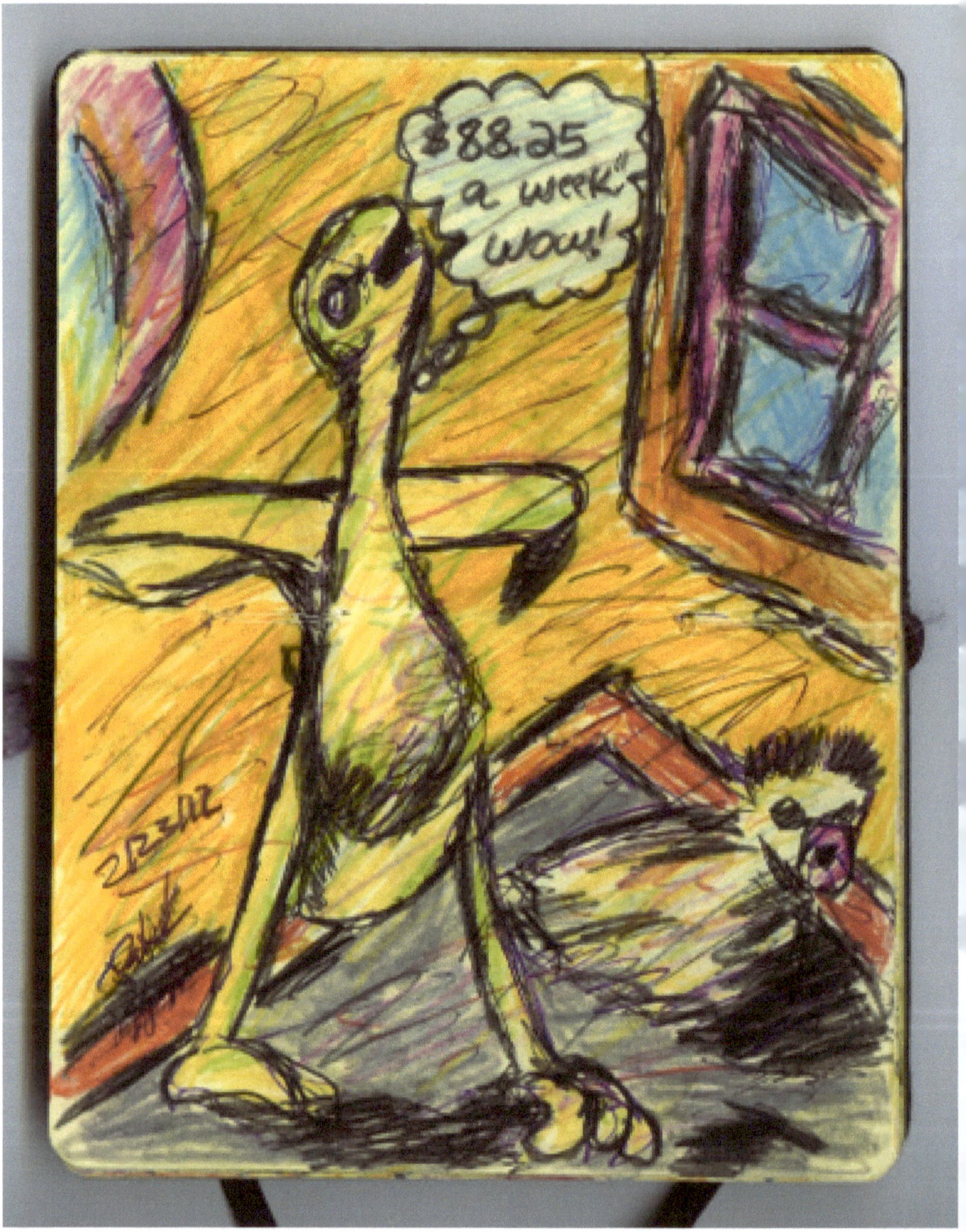
$88.25 a week" wow!

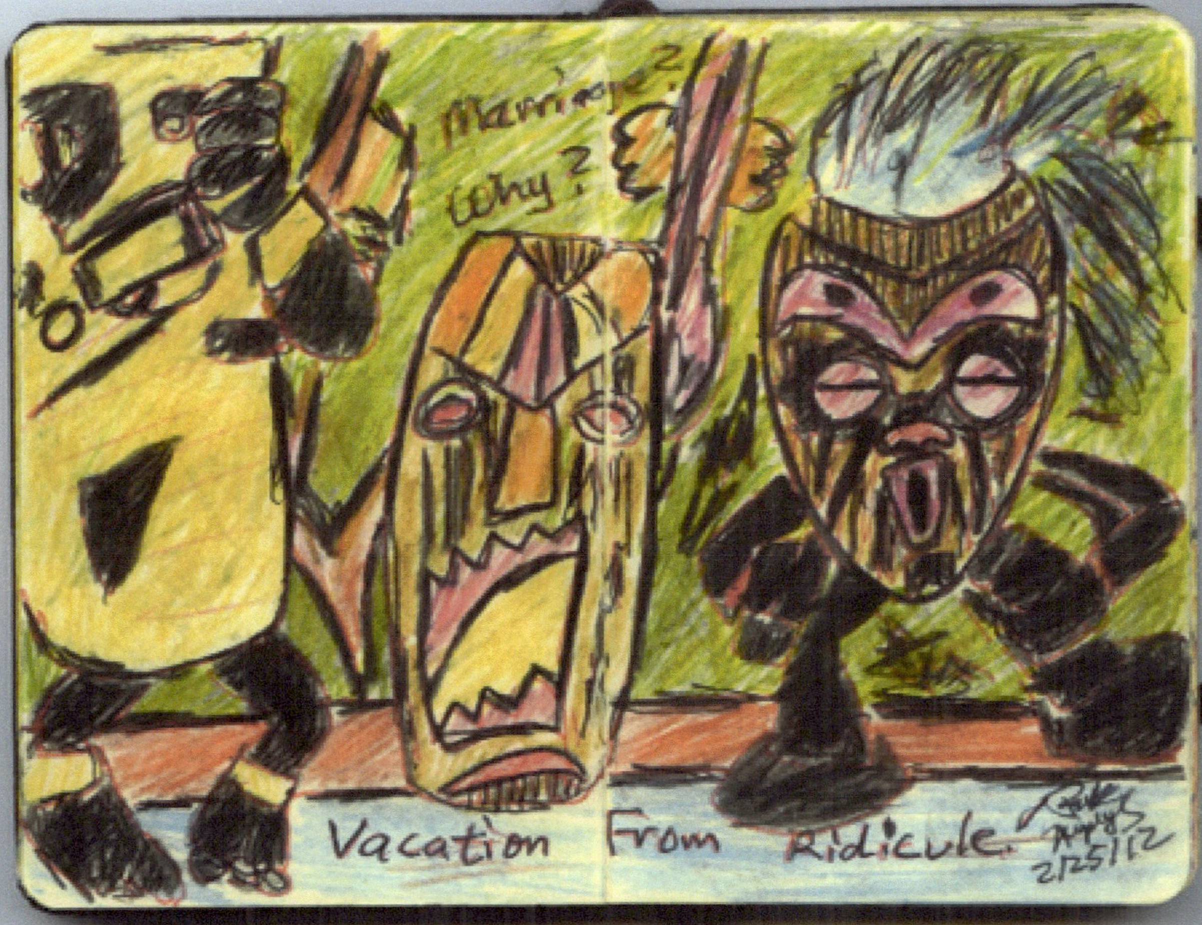
Marriage?
Why?
Vacation From Ridicule.
2/25/12

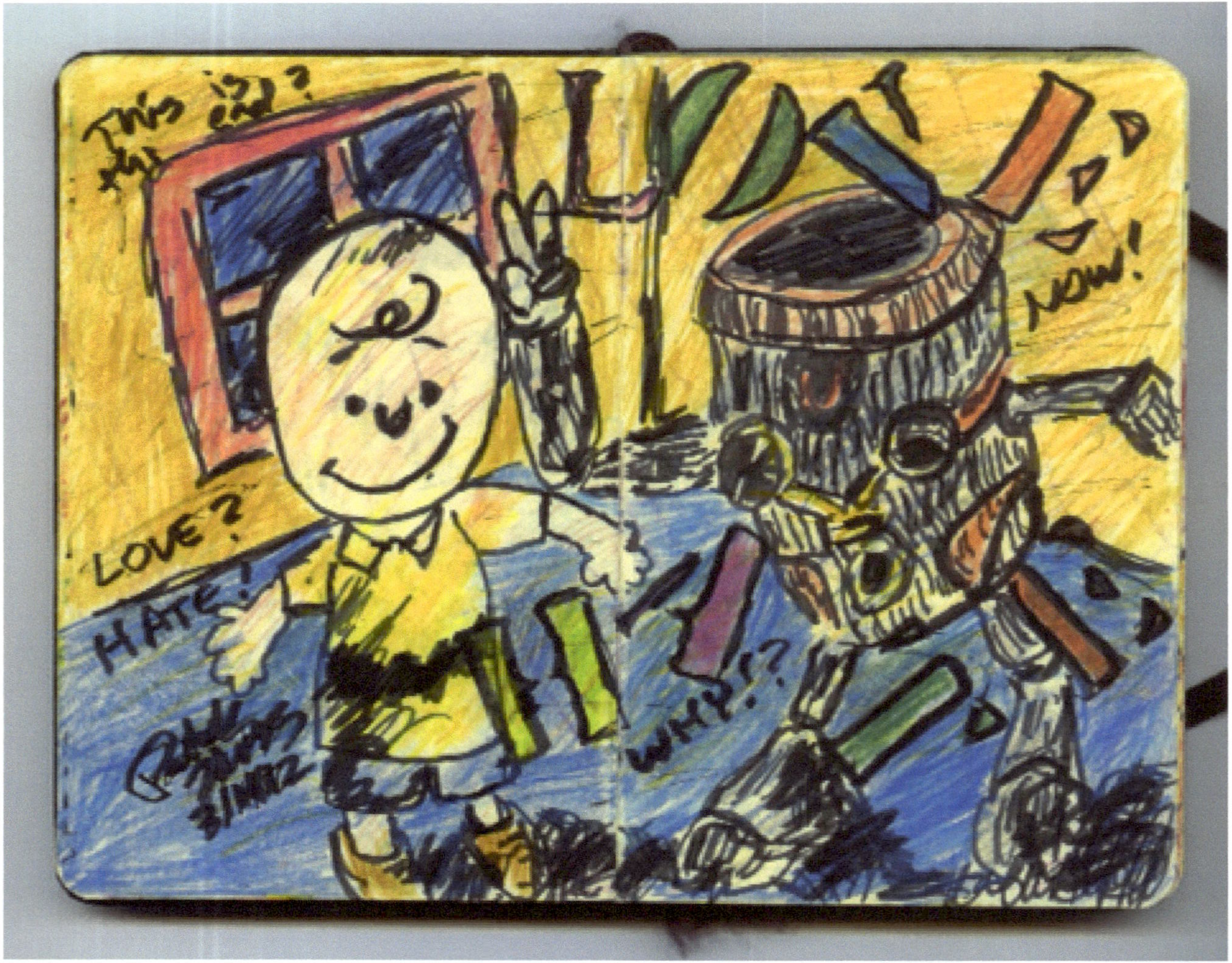
This is the end?
LOVE?
HATE!
WHY!?
NOW!

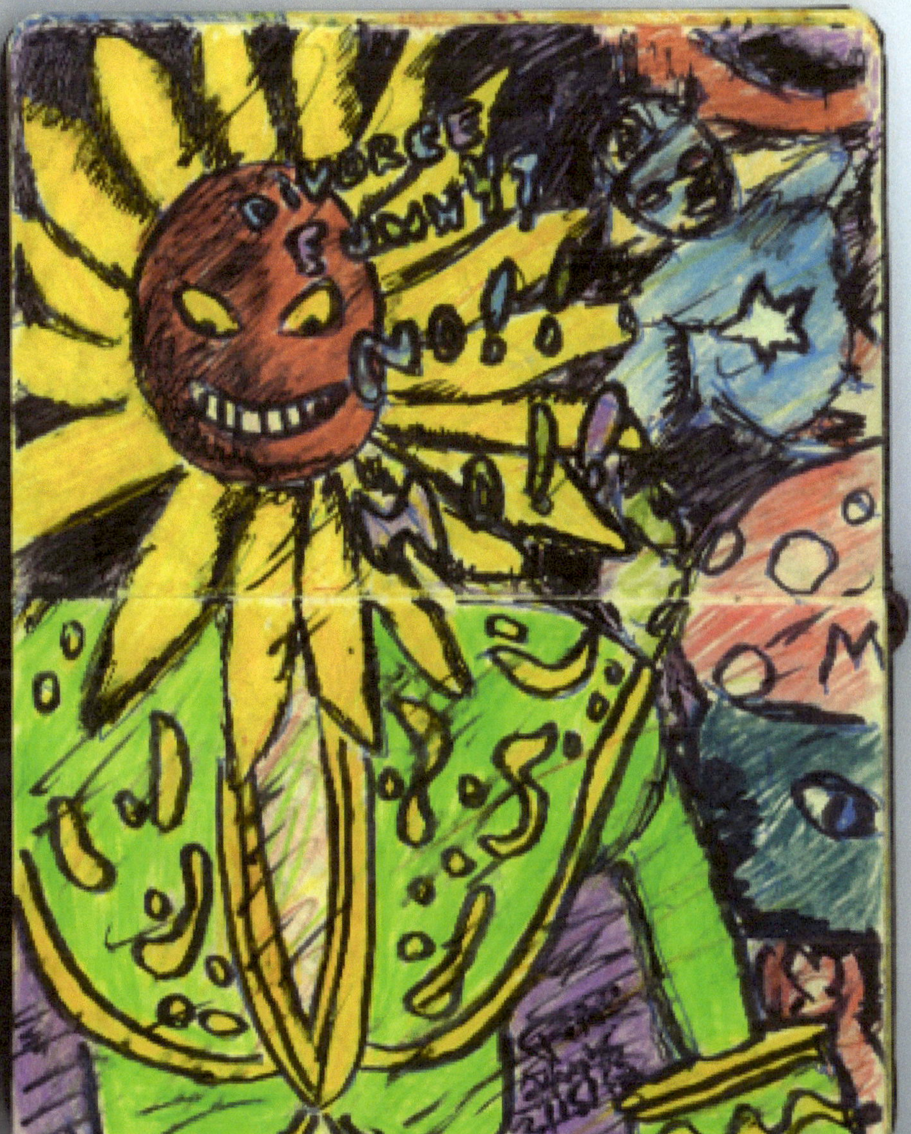
DIVORCE
FUNNY!
NO!!

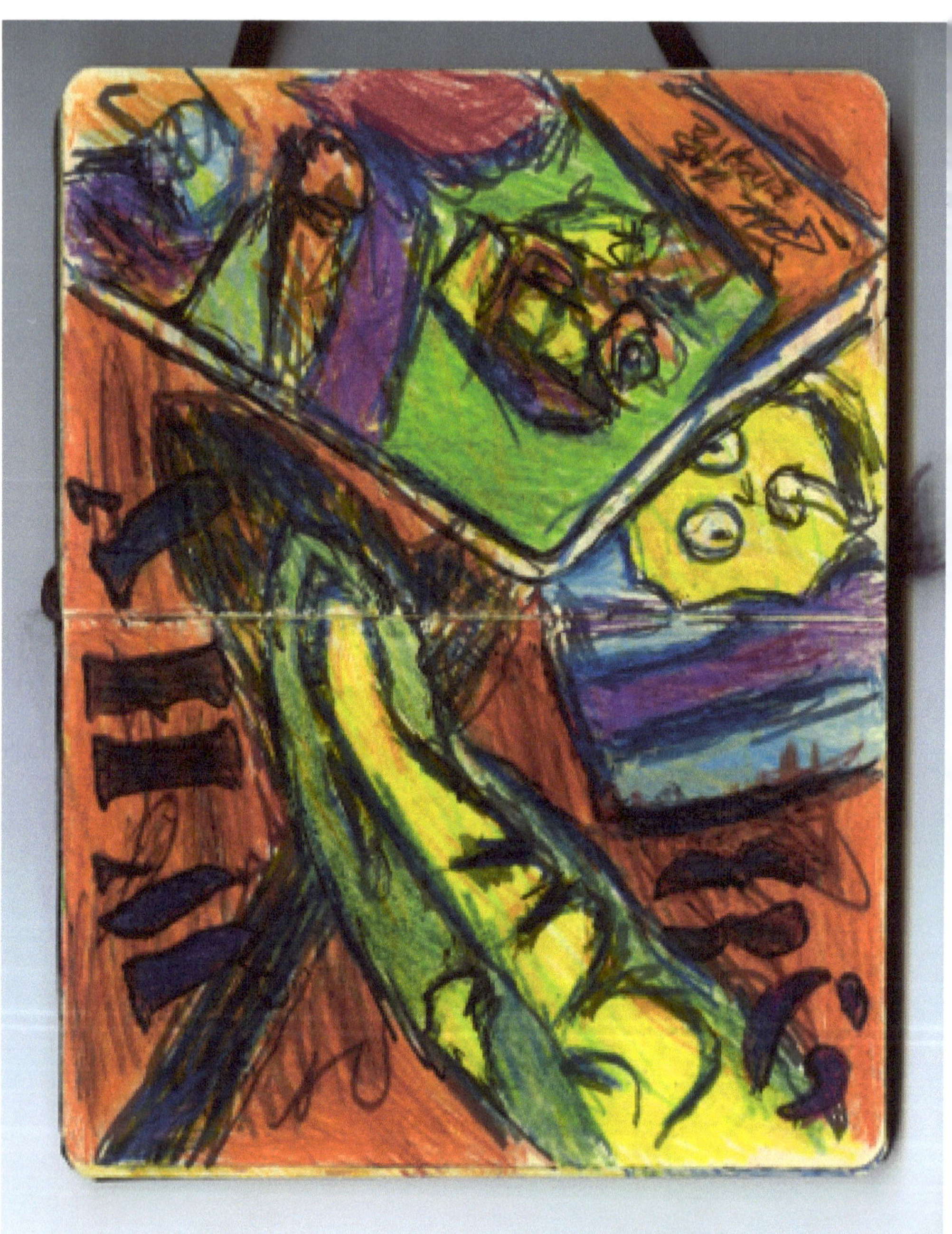

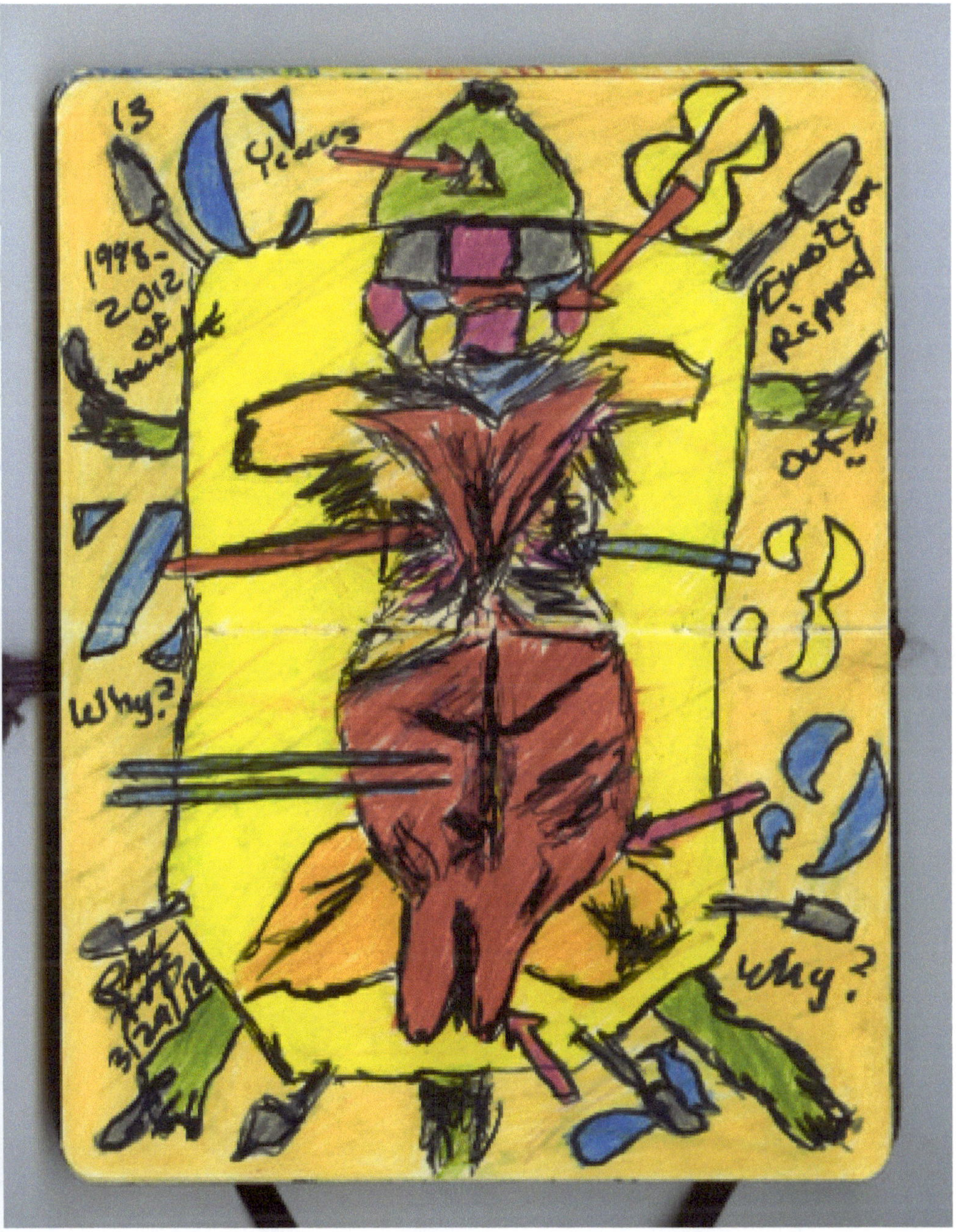
13
years
1998-2012
of torment
Emotion Ripped out!!
Why?
why?

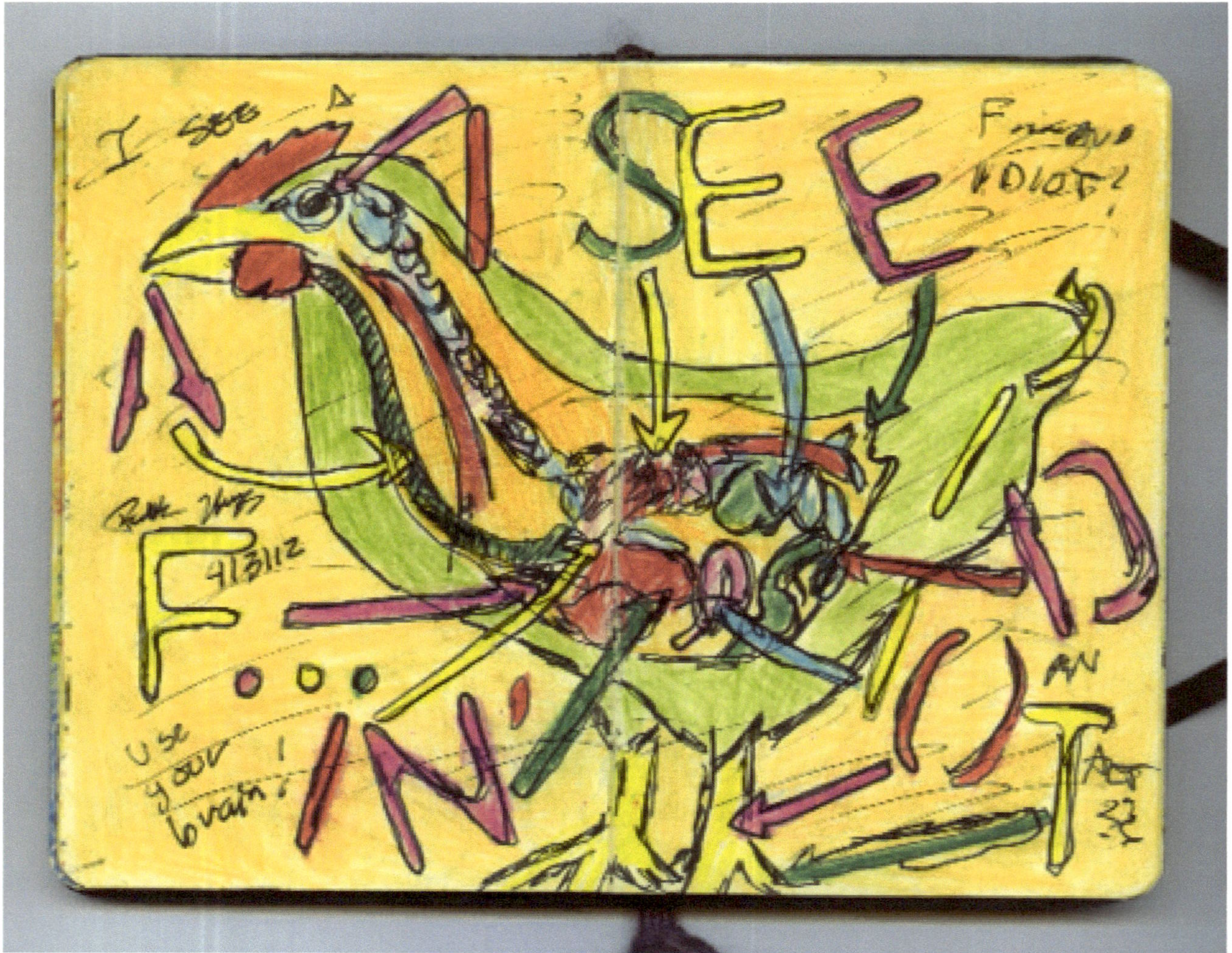
I see a
SEE
F...
4/3/12
Use your brain!
an

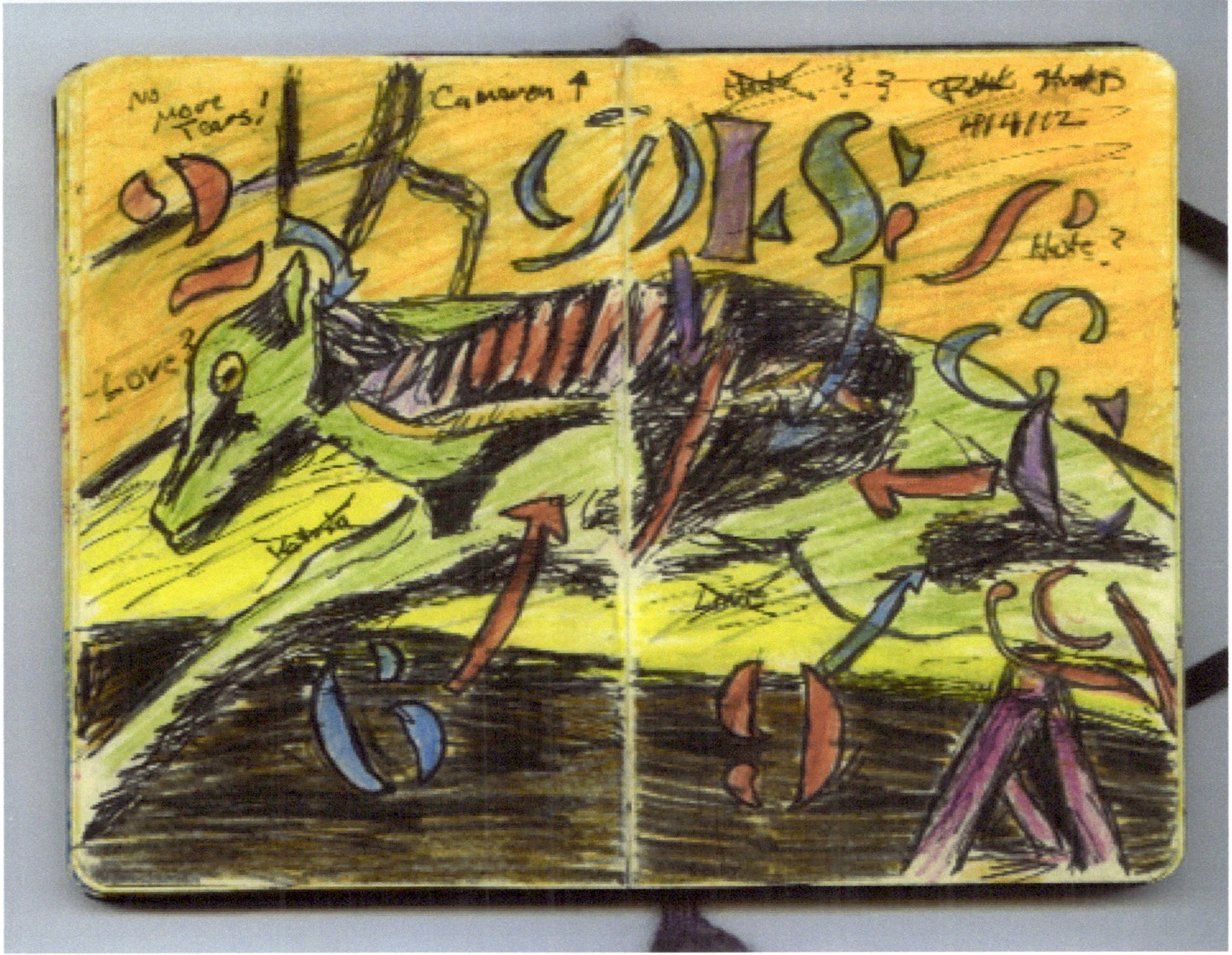

No more Tears!
Cameron ↑
Love?
Hate?
4/14/12

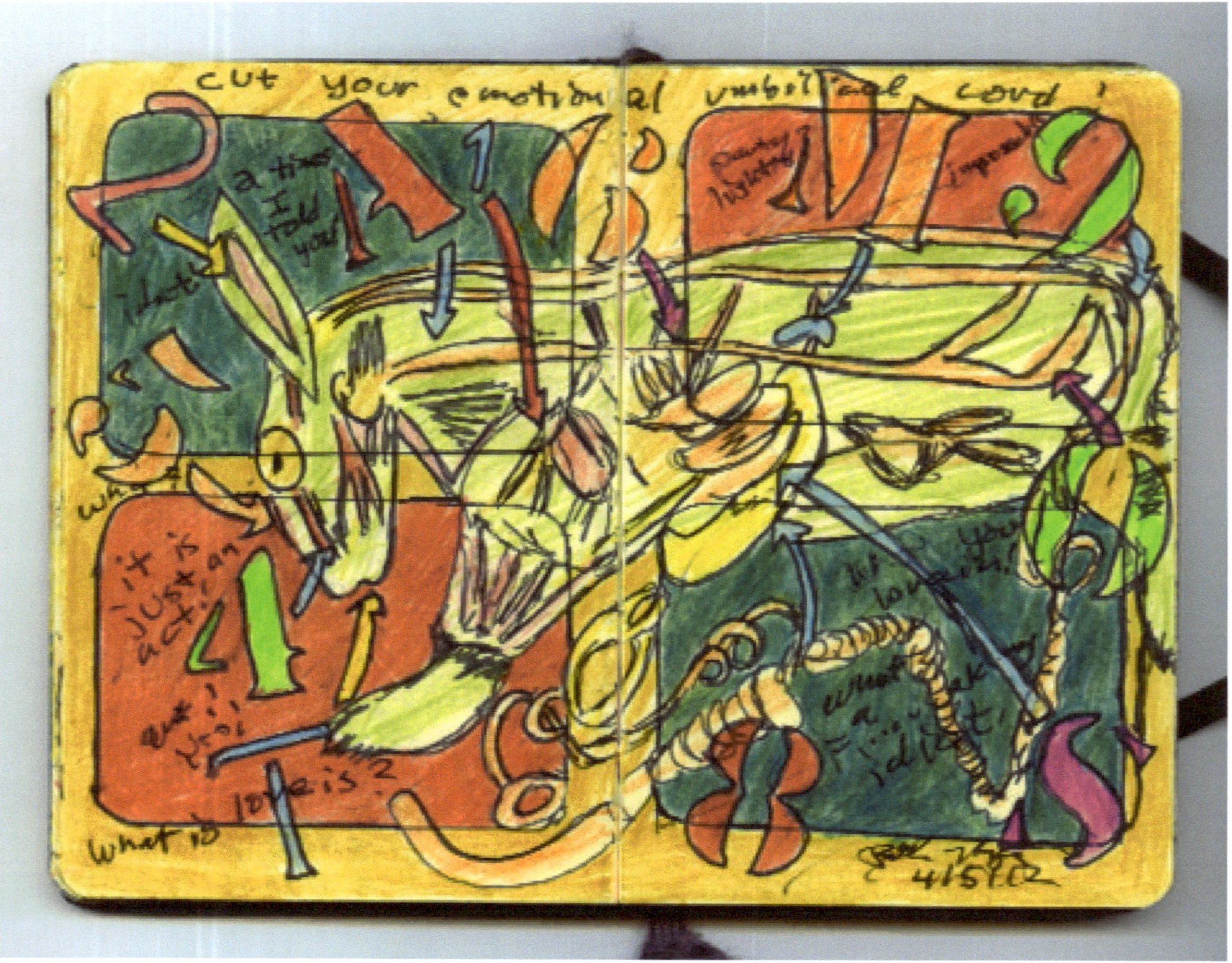
cut your emotional umbilical cord!
it is just an act!
4/5/12

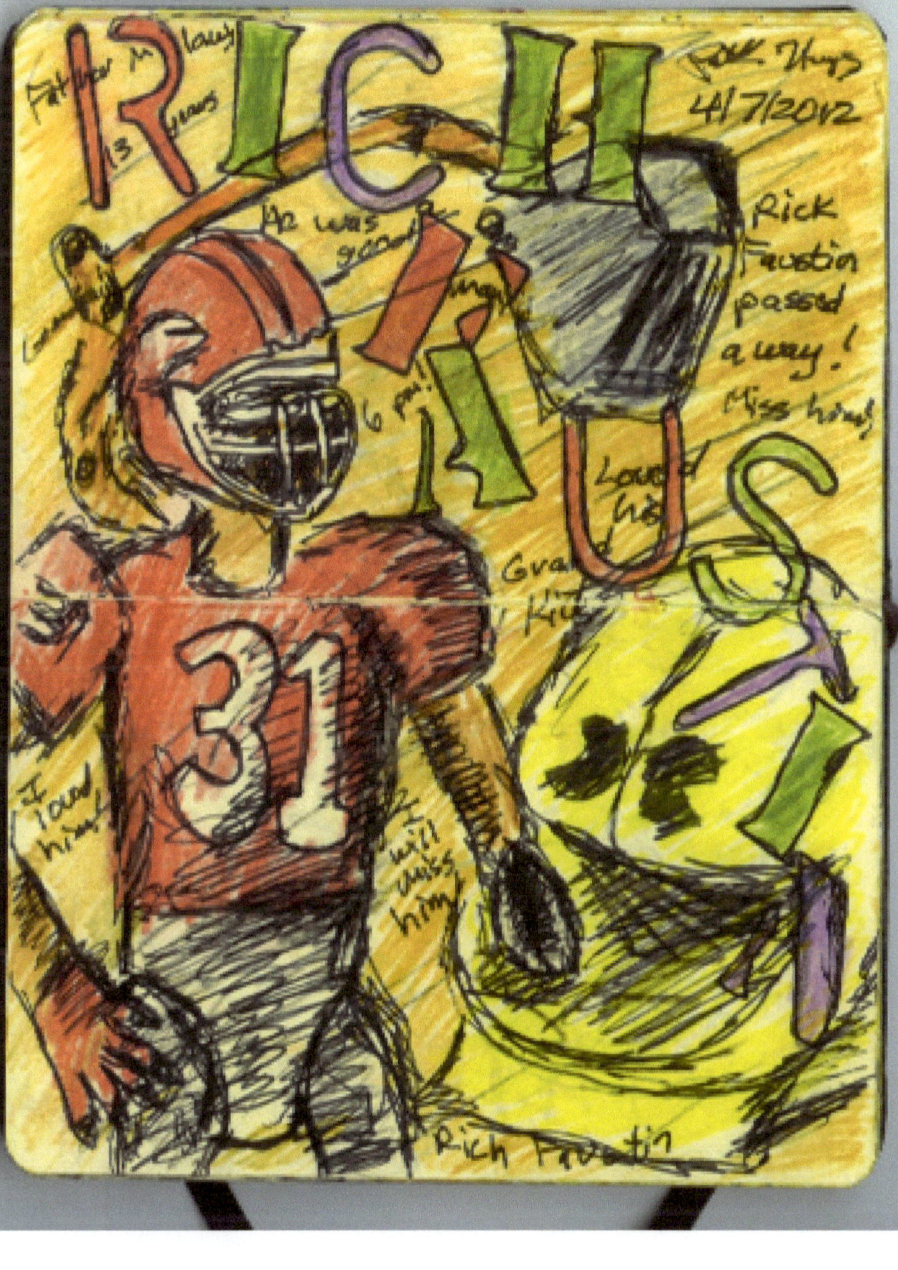
Father in law
13 years
4/7/2012
Rick
Faustin
passed
a way!
Miss him!
He was
good
I loved
him
I
will
miss
him
31
Rich Faustin

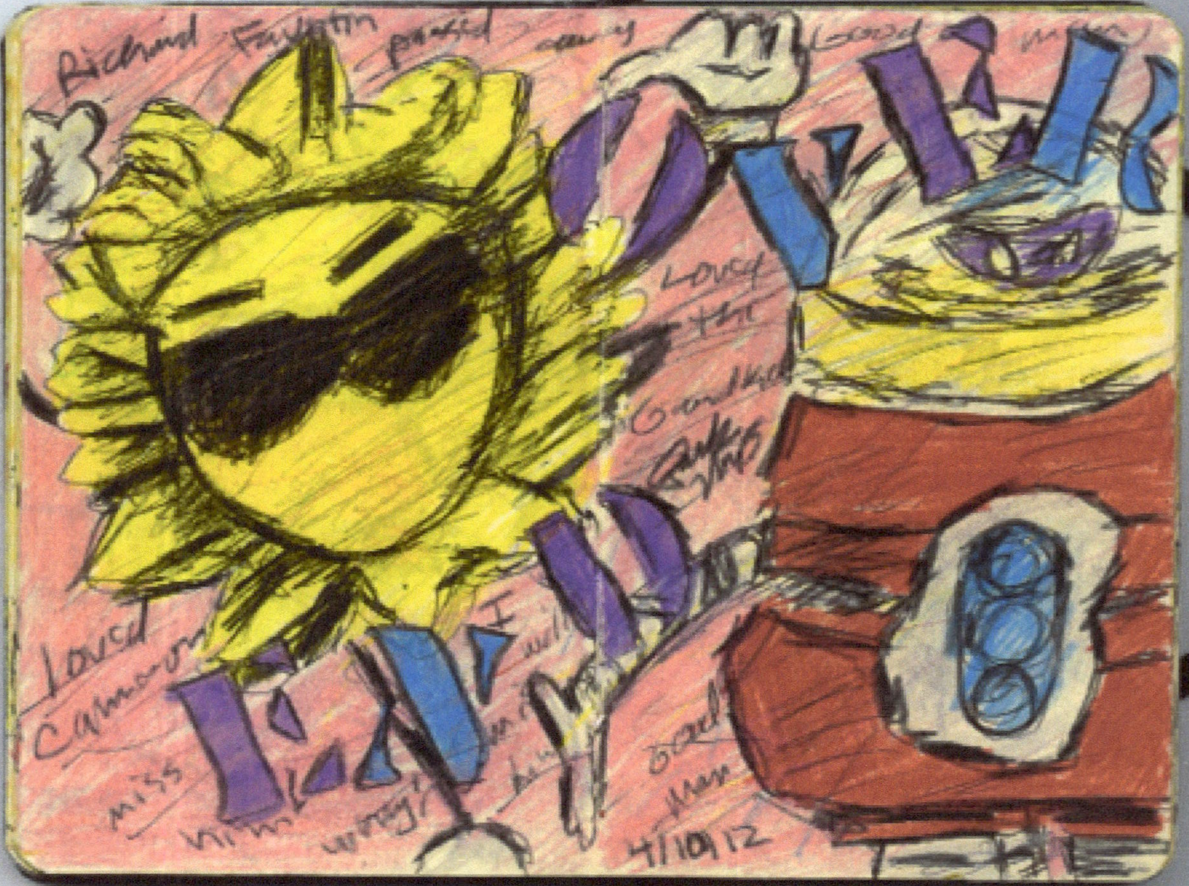
Loved the
4/10/12

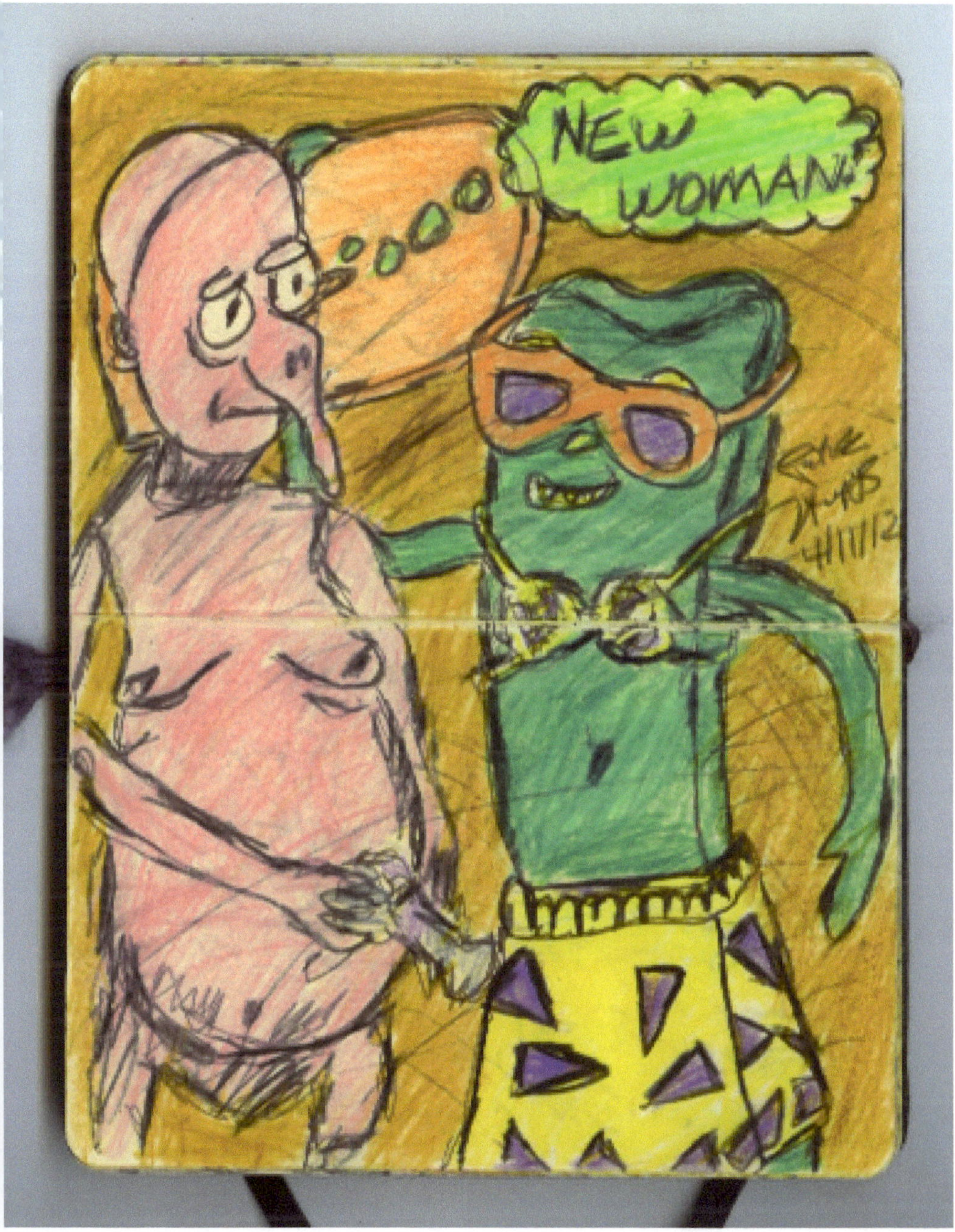
NEW WOMAN!

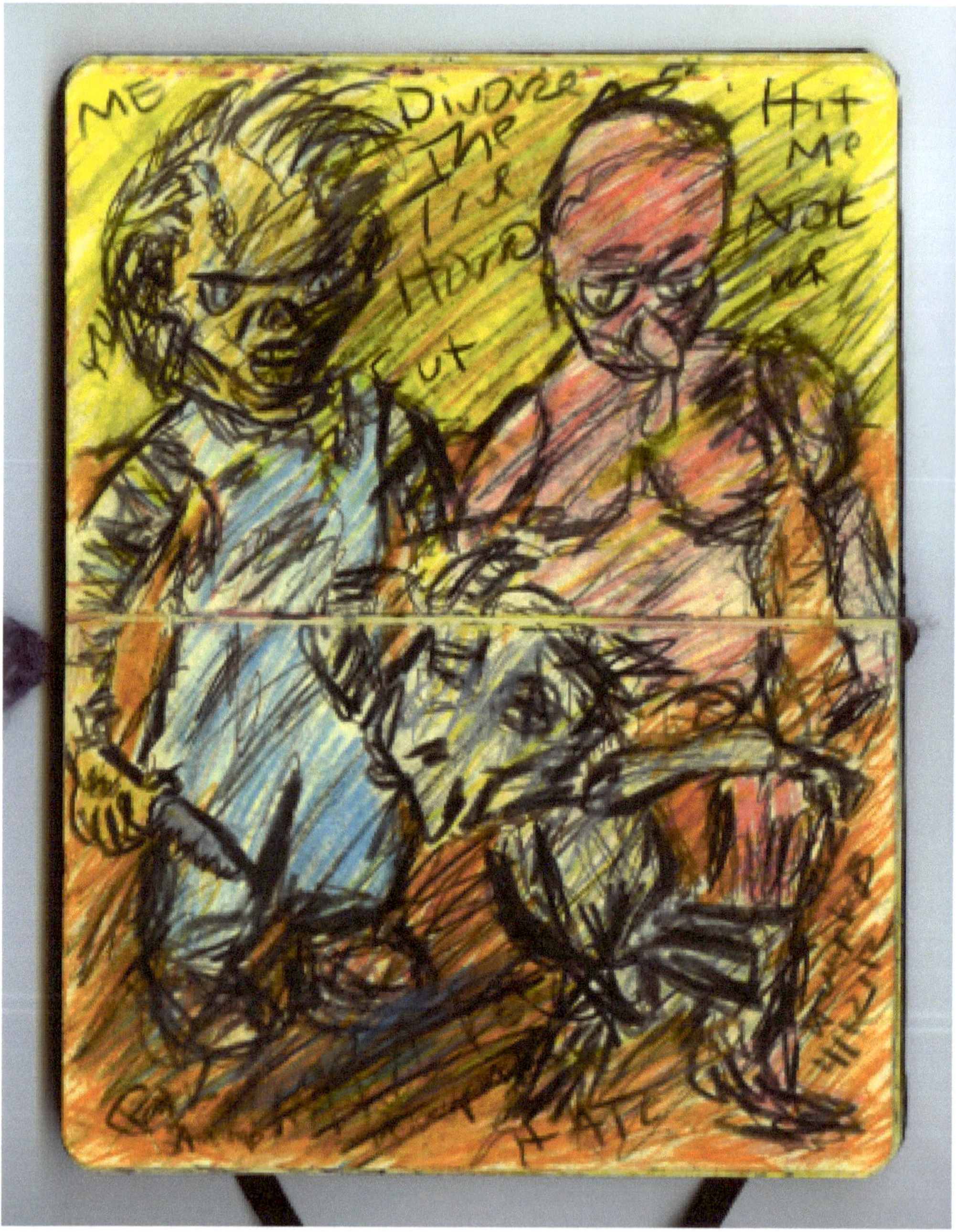
ME
Divorce
The
Hit
Me
Not

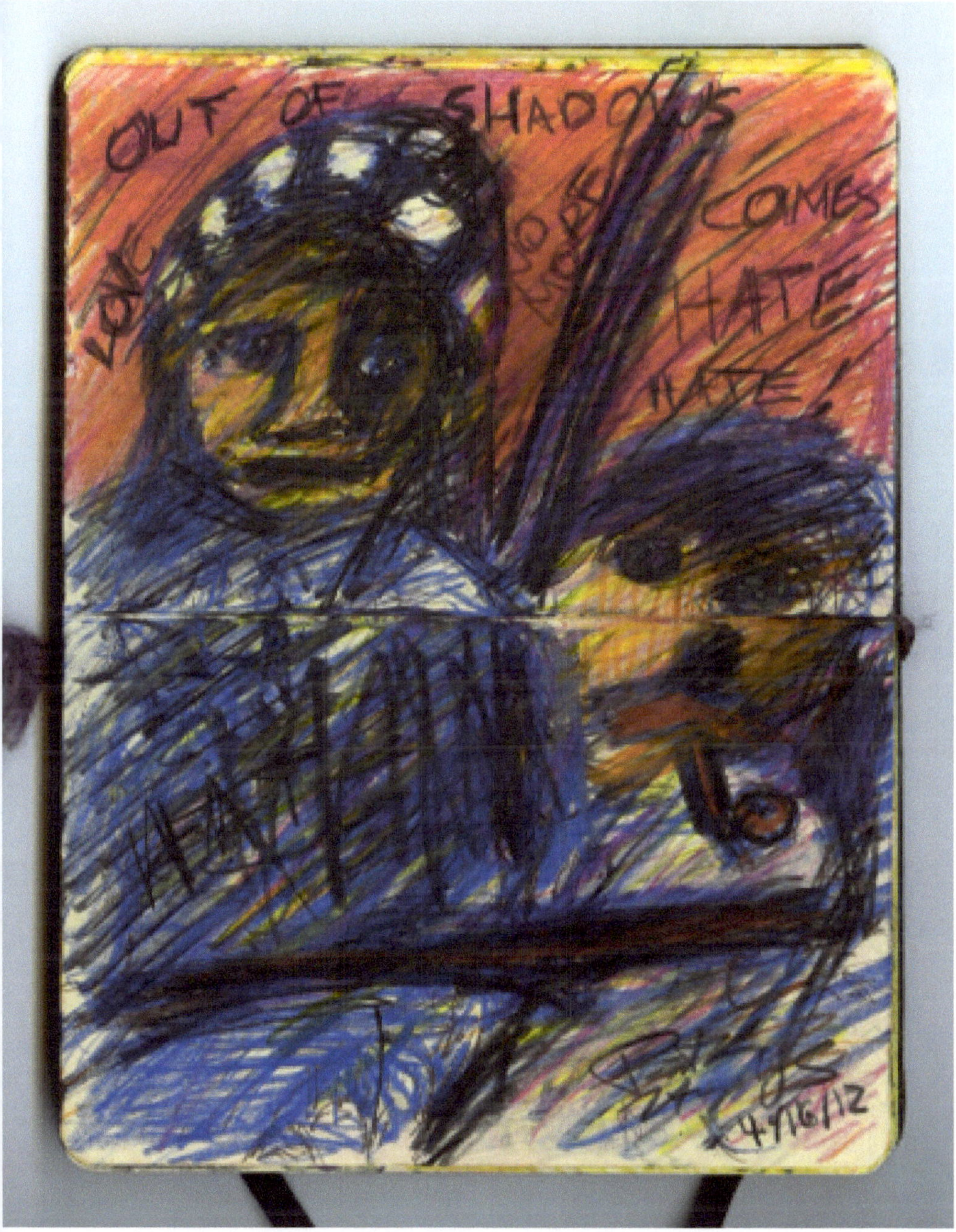
OUT OF SHADOWS
LOVE
COMES
HATE
HATE!
4/16/12

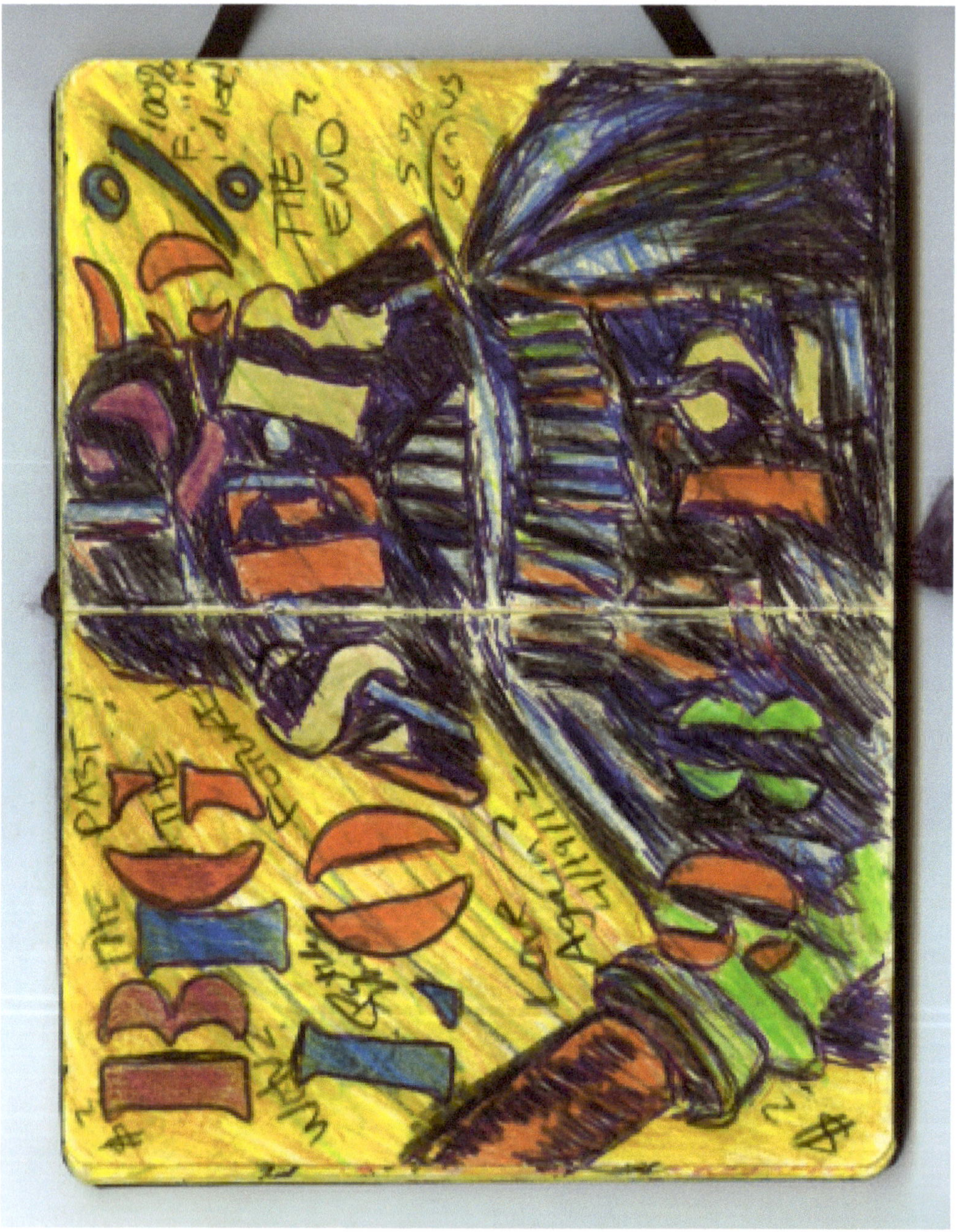
THE END

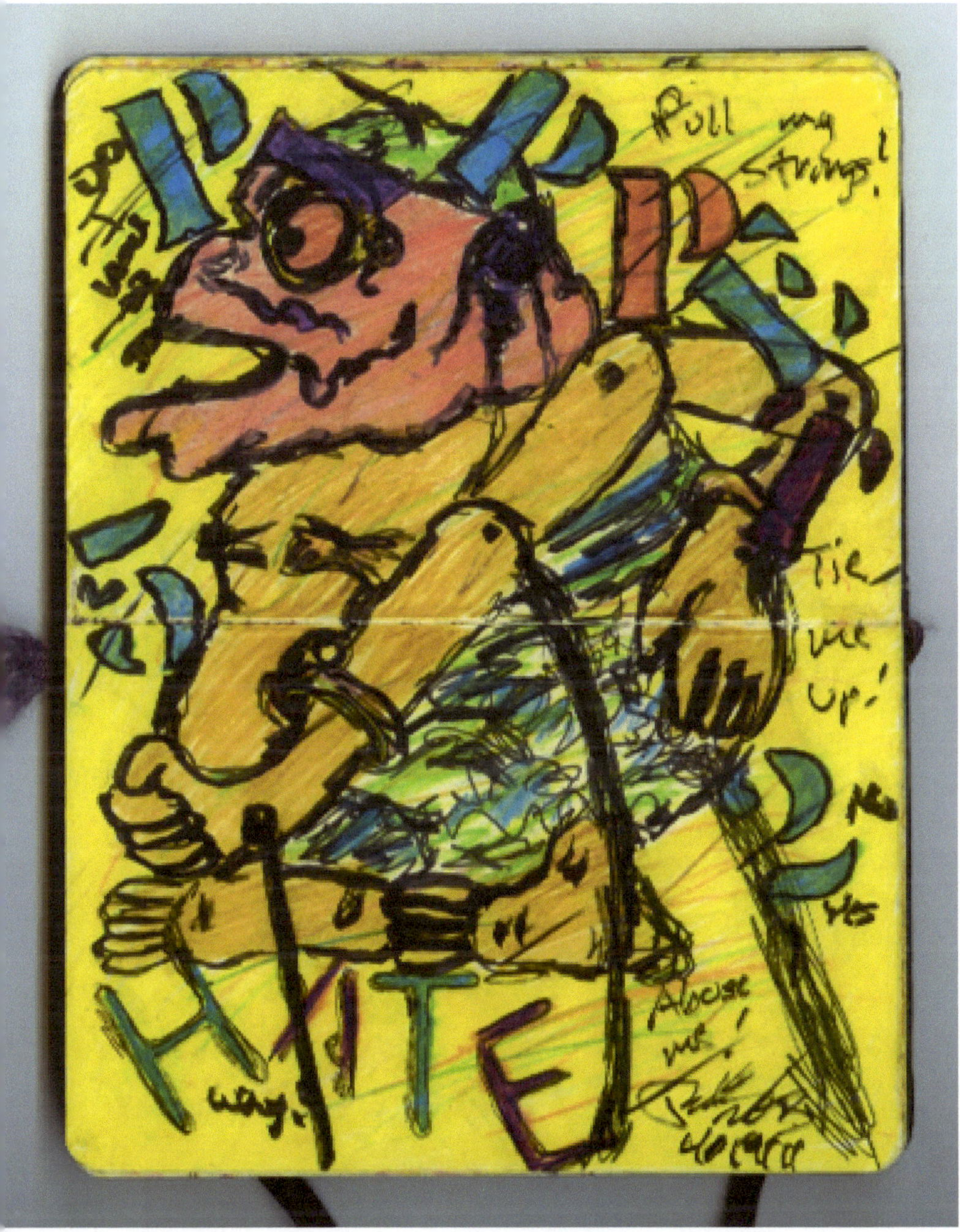
Pull my Strings!
Tie me up!
Abuse me!

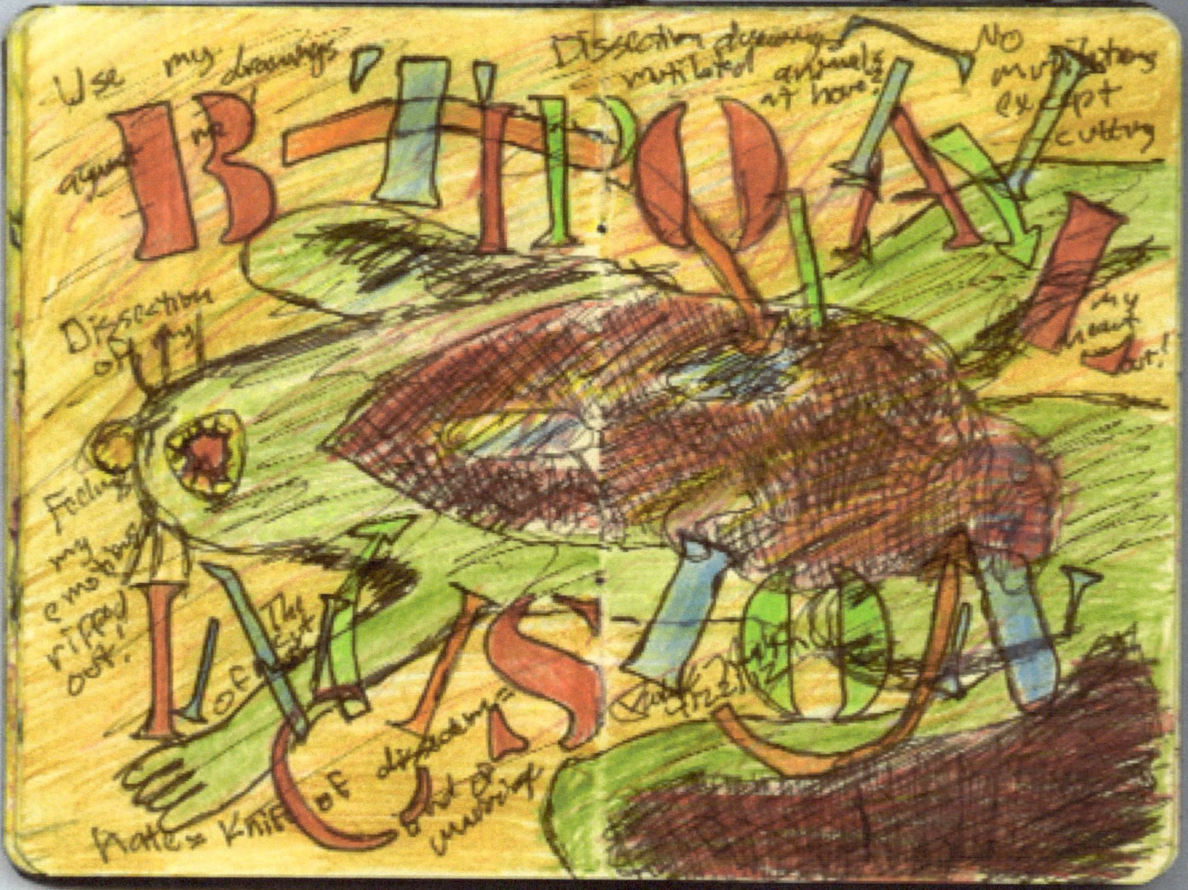
Use my drawings
Dissection drawings mutilated animals at home!
No mutilations except cutting
Feeling my emotions ripped out!
my heart out!

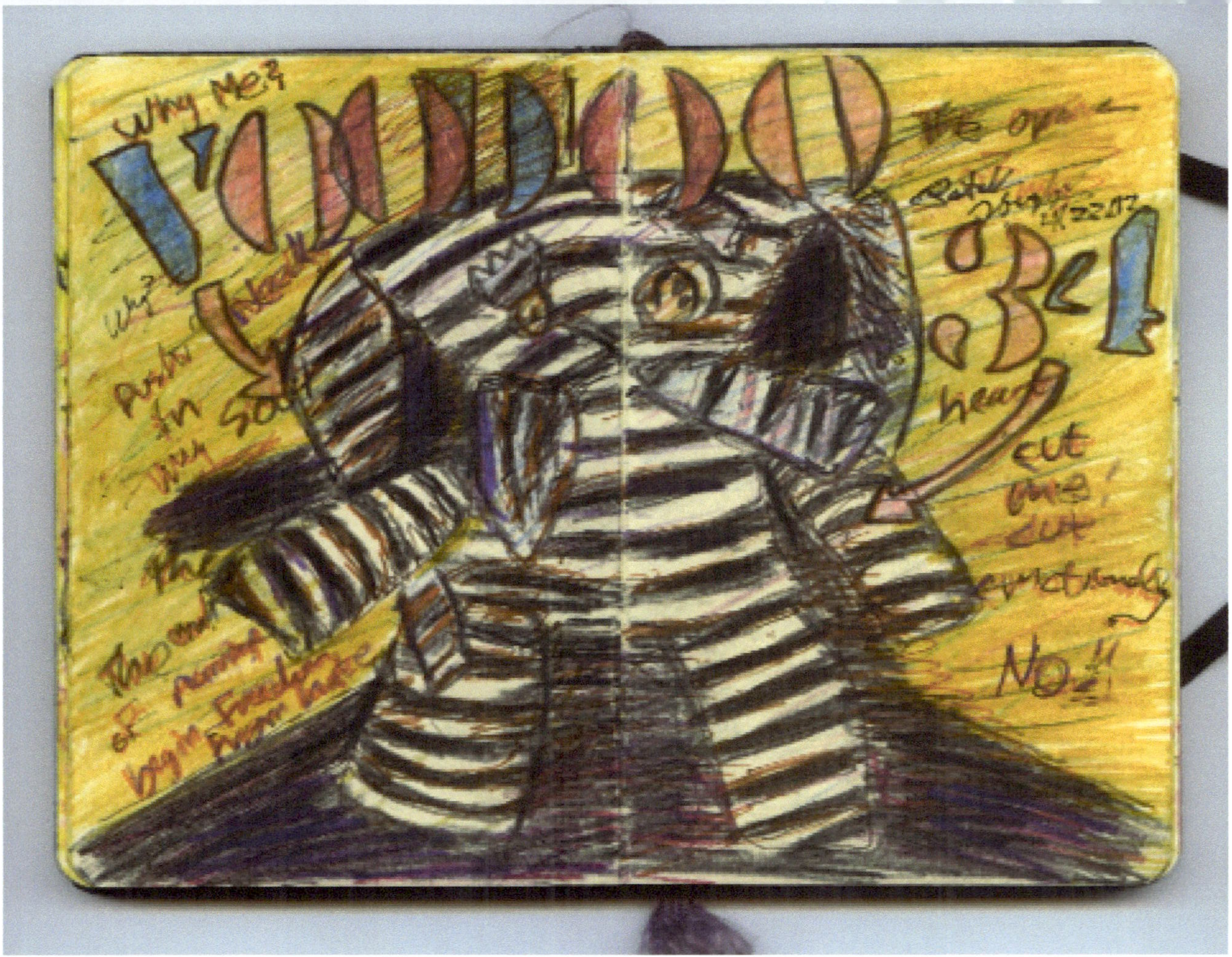

Why Me?
heart
cut me!
cut
emotionally
NO!!

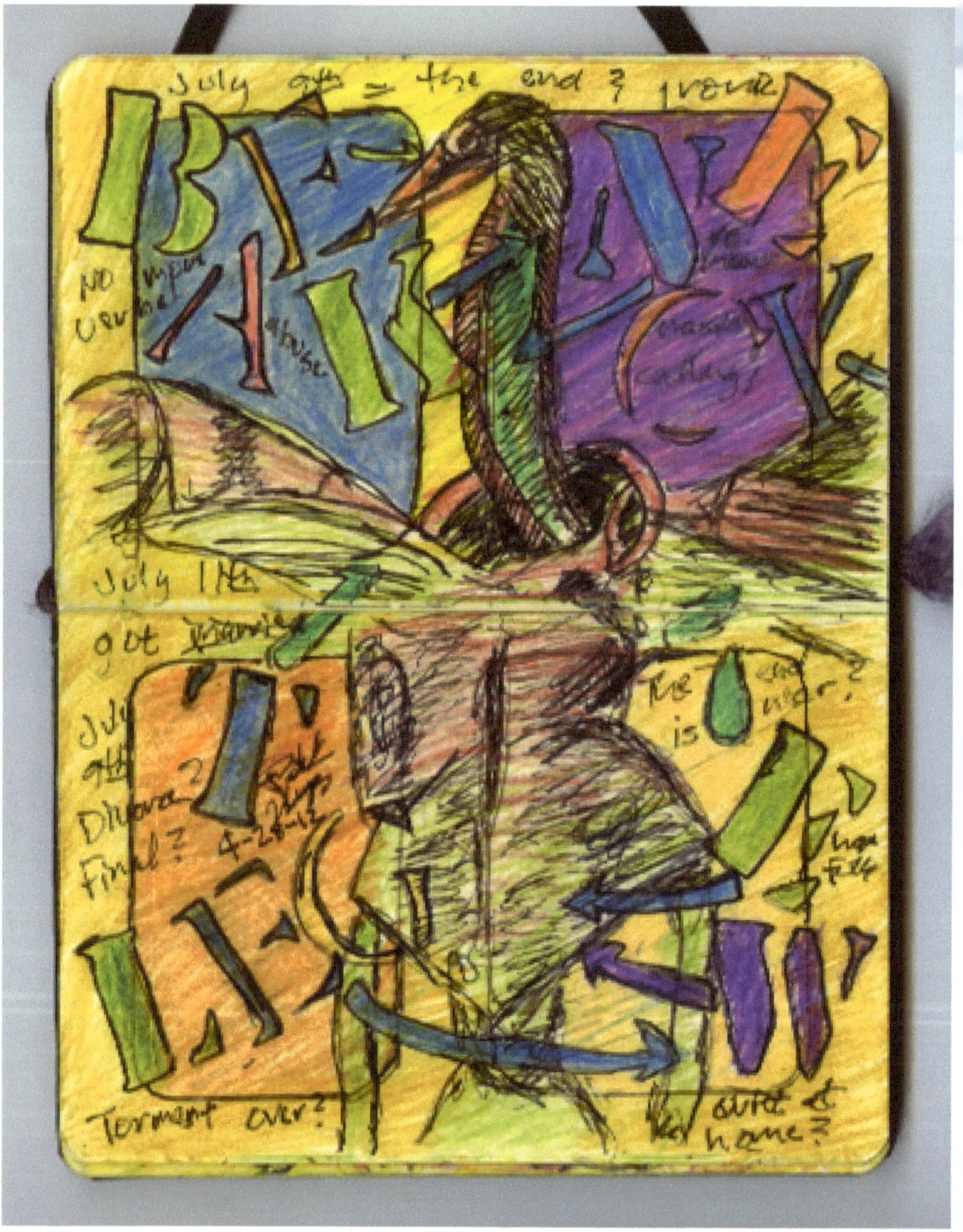

Torment over?

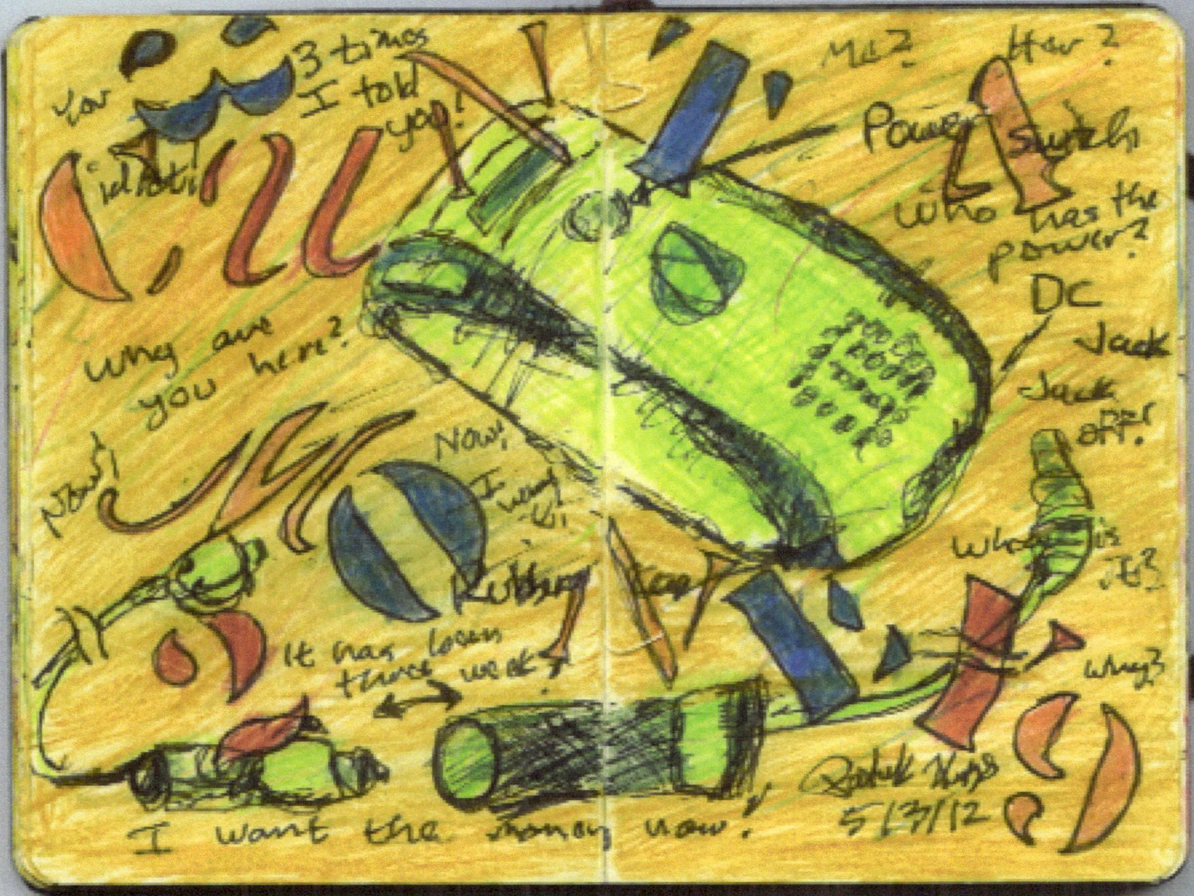
3 times
I told
you!
Me?
Her?
Power switch
Who has the
power?
DC
Jack
Jack
off.
Why are
you here?
Now!
Now,
Who is
it?
Why?
It has been
three weeks
I want the money now!
5/3/12

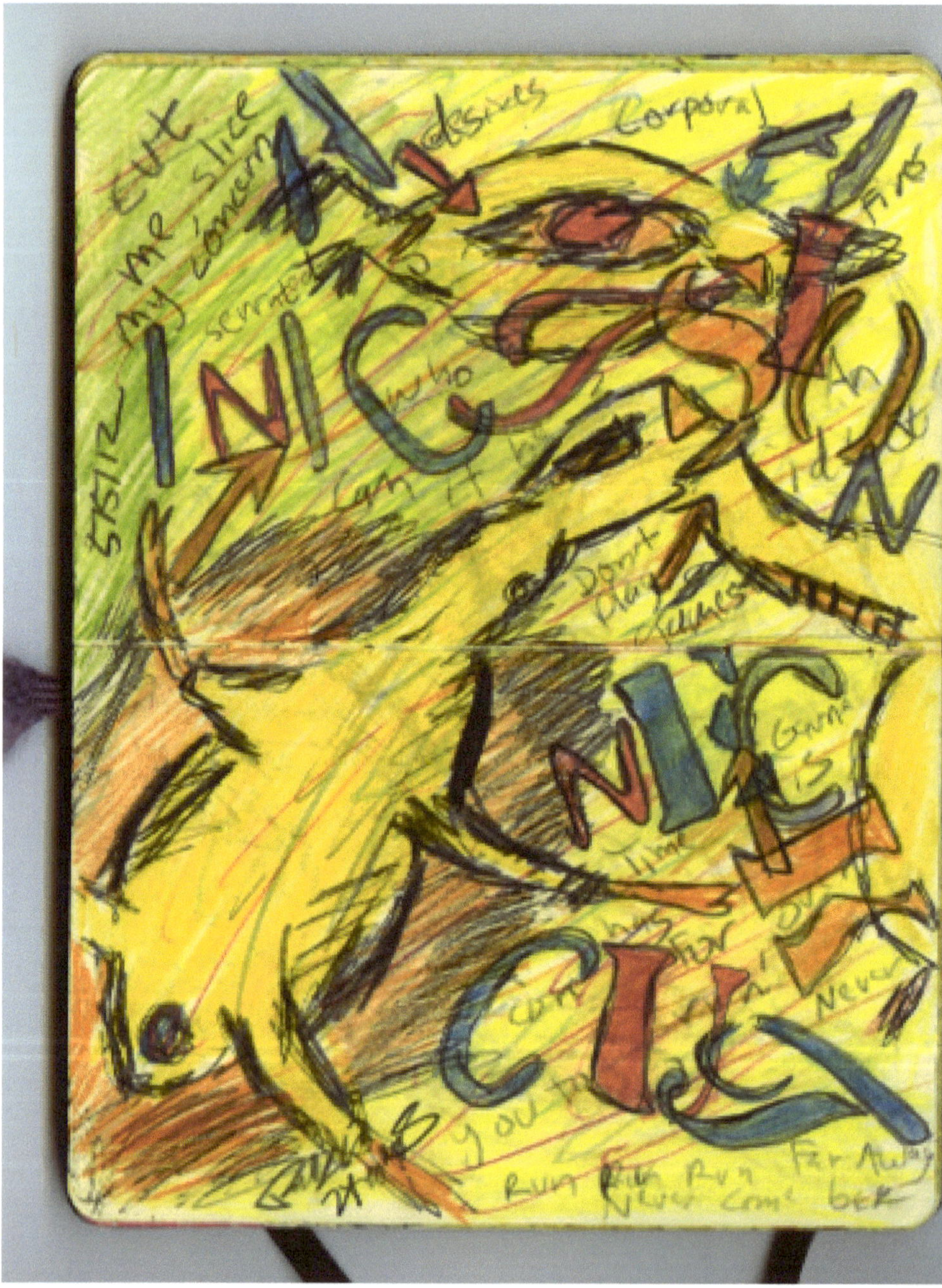
Cut me slice
my concern
desires
Corporal
Never
Run Run Run
Never come bck
Far Away

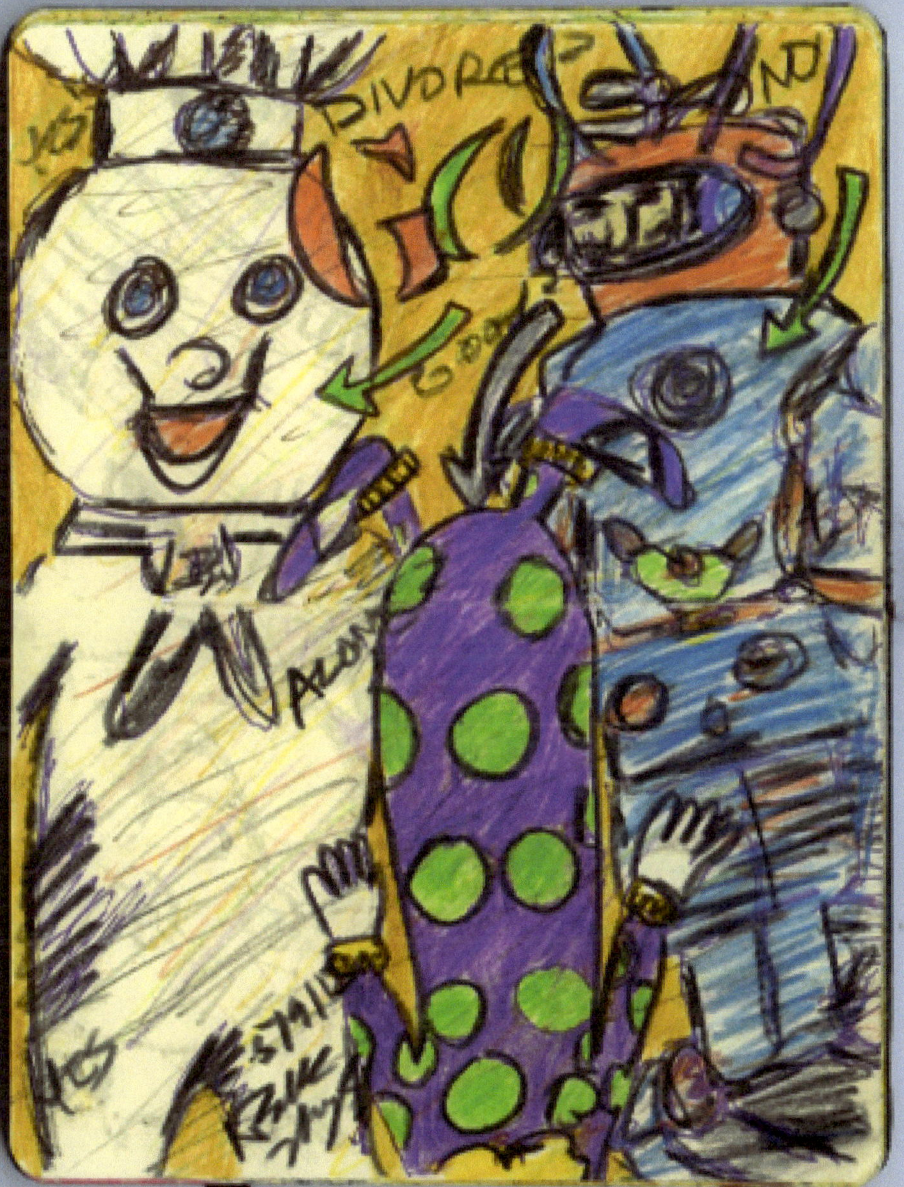
DIVORCE?
NO

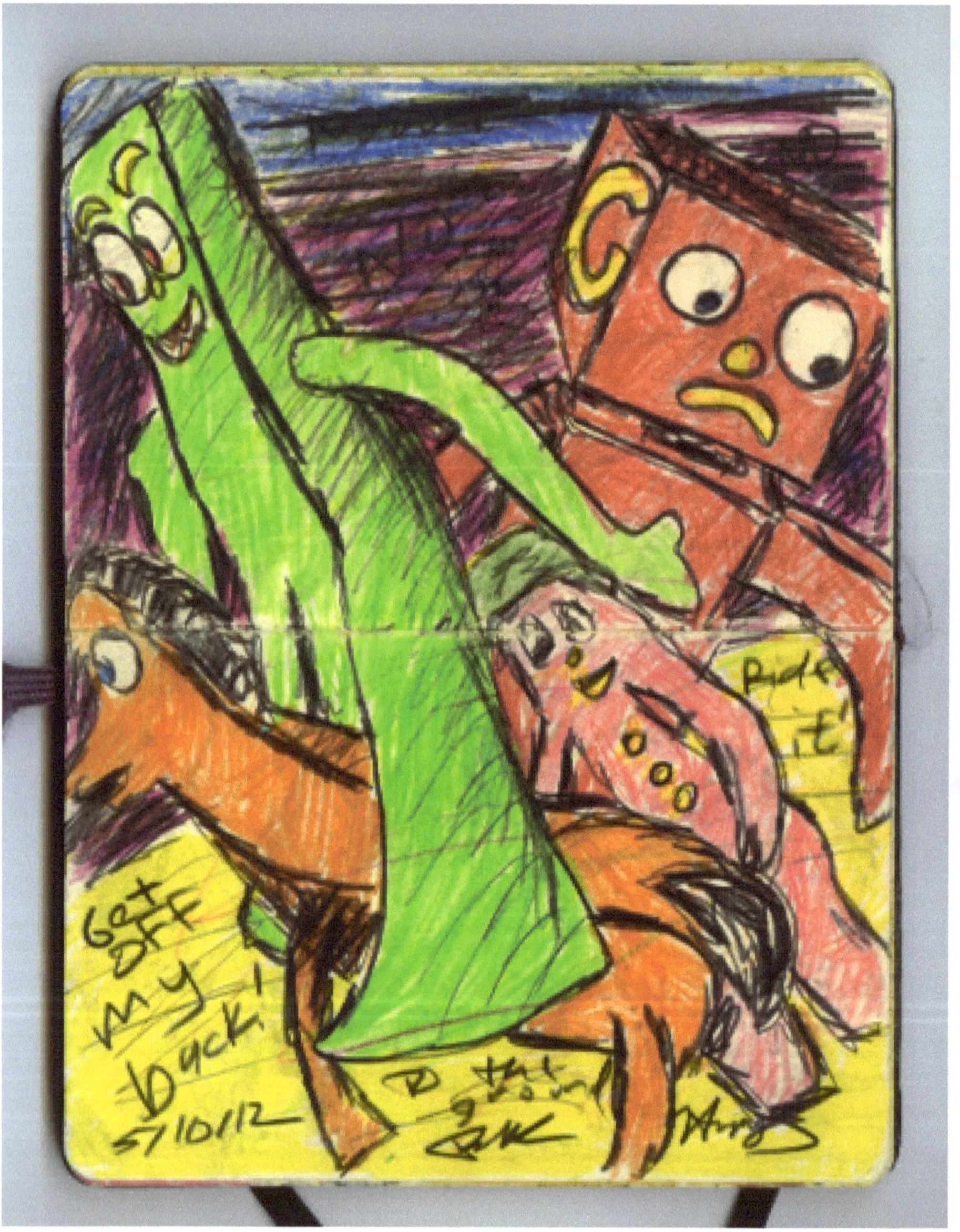

Ride it!
Get OFF my back!
5/10/12

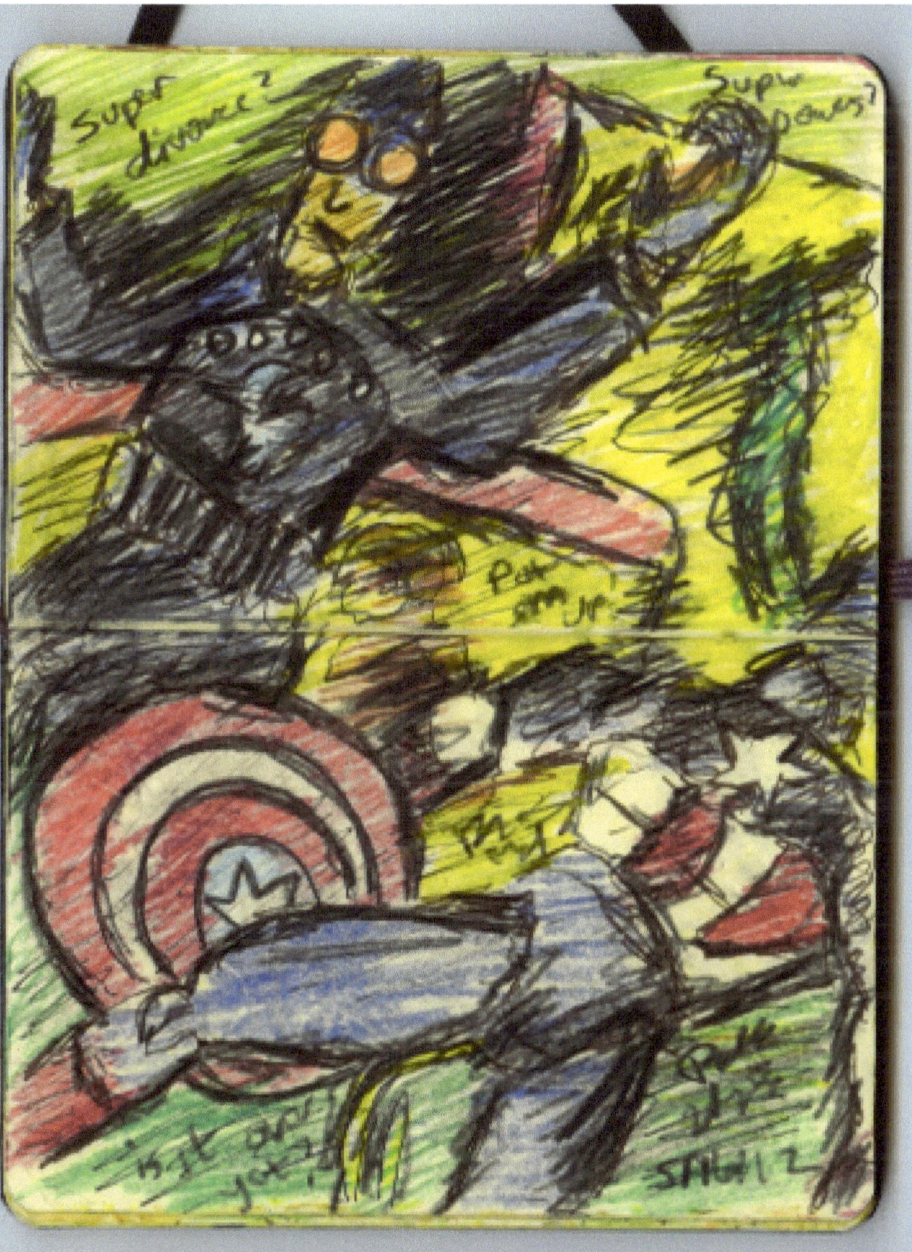
Super divorce?
Super powers?

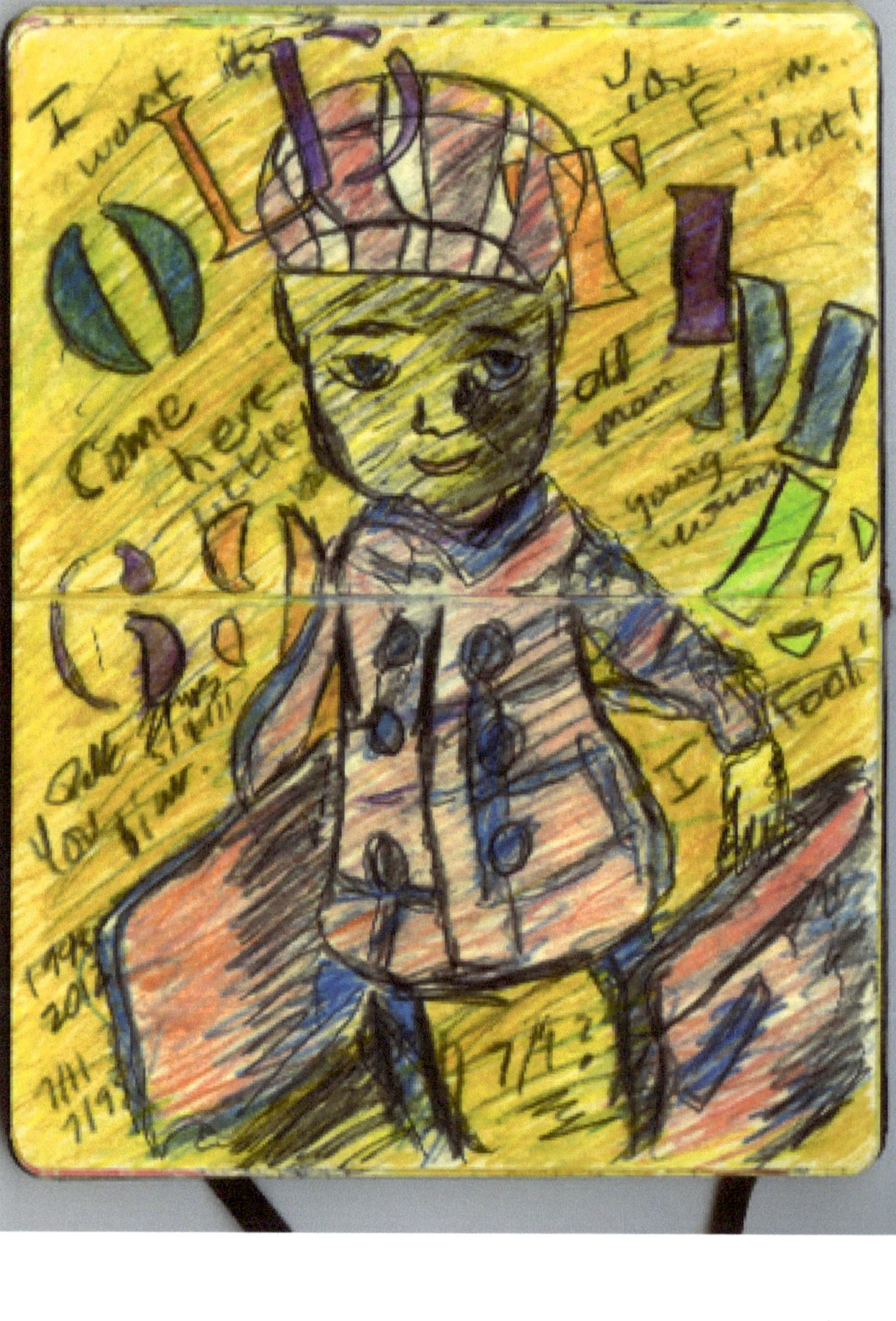
I want it
idiot!
Come here
old man
Fool!

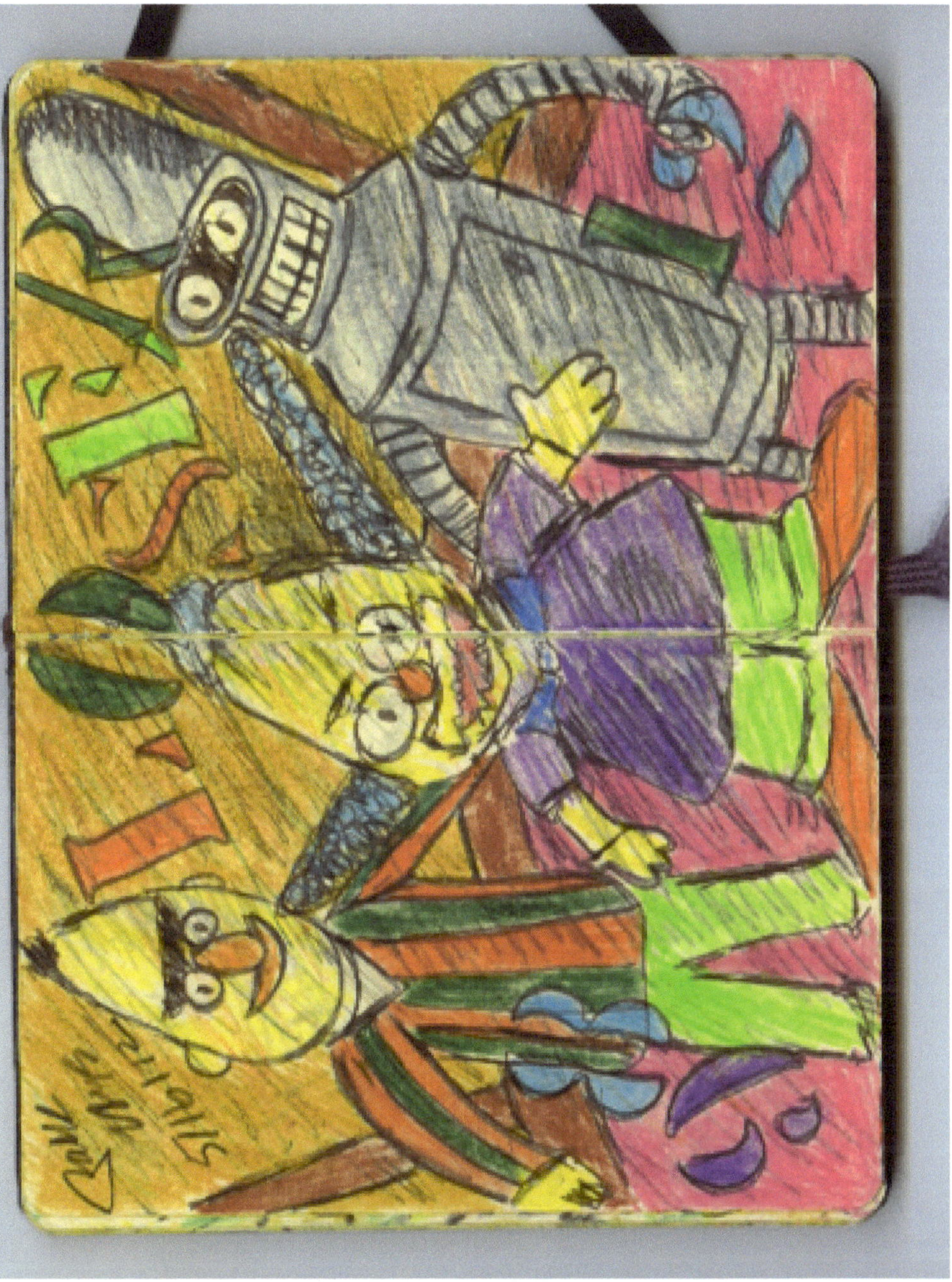

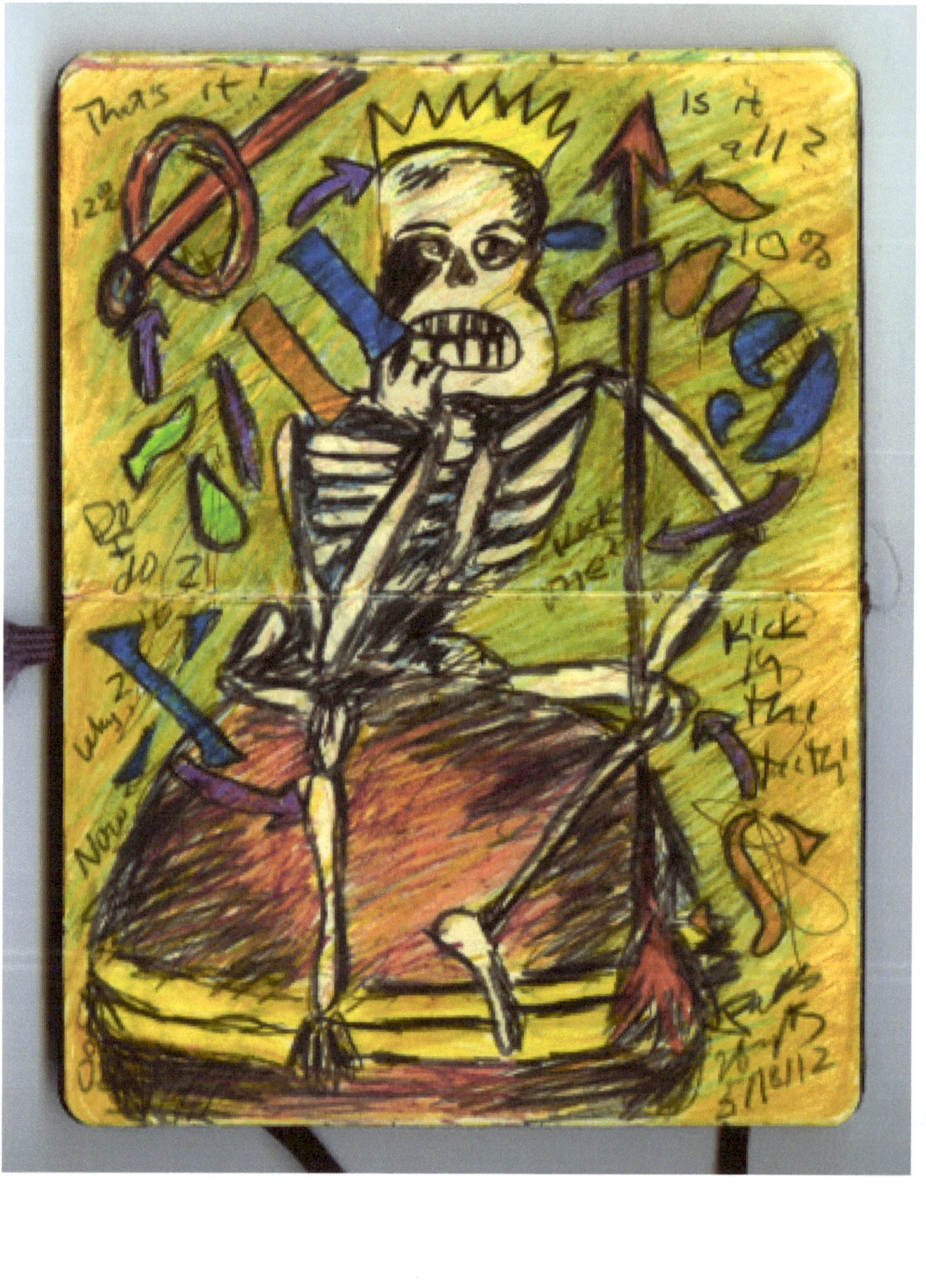
That's it!
is it all?
10%
Kick me!
Kick in the teeth!

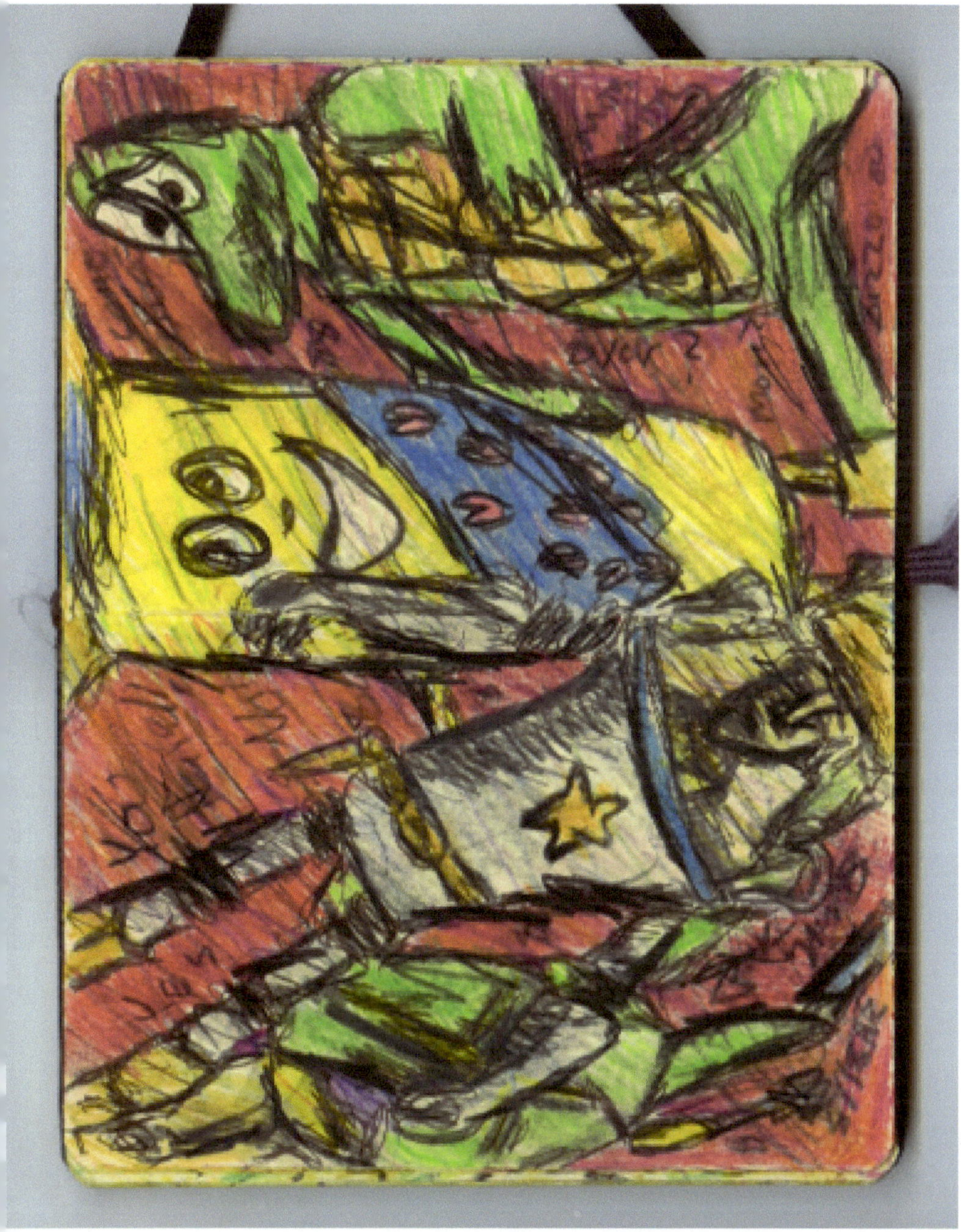

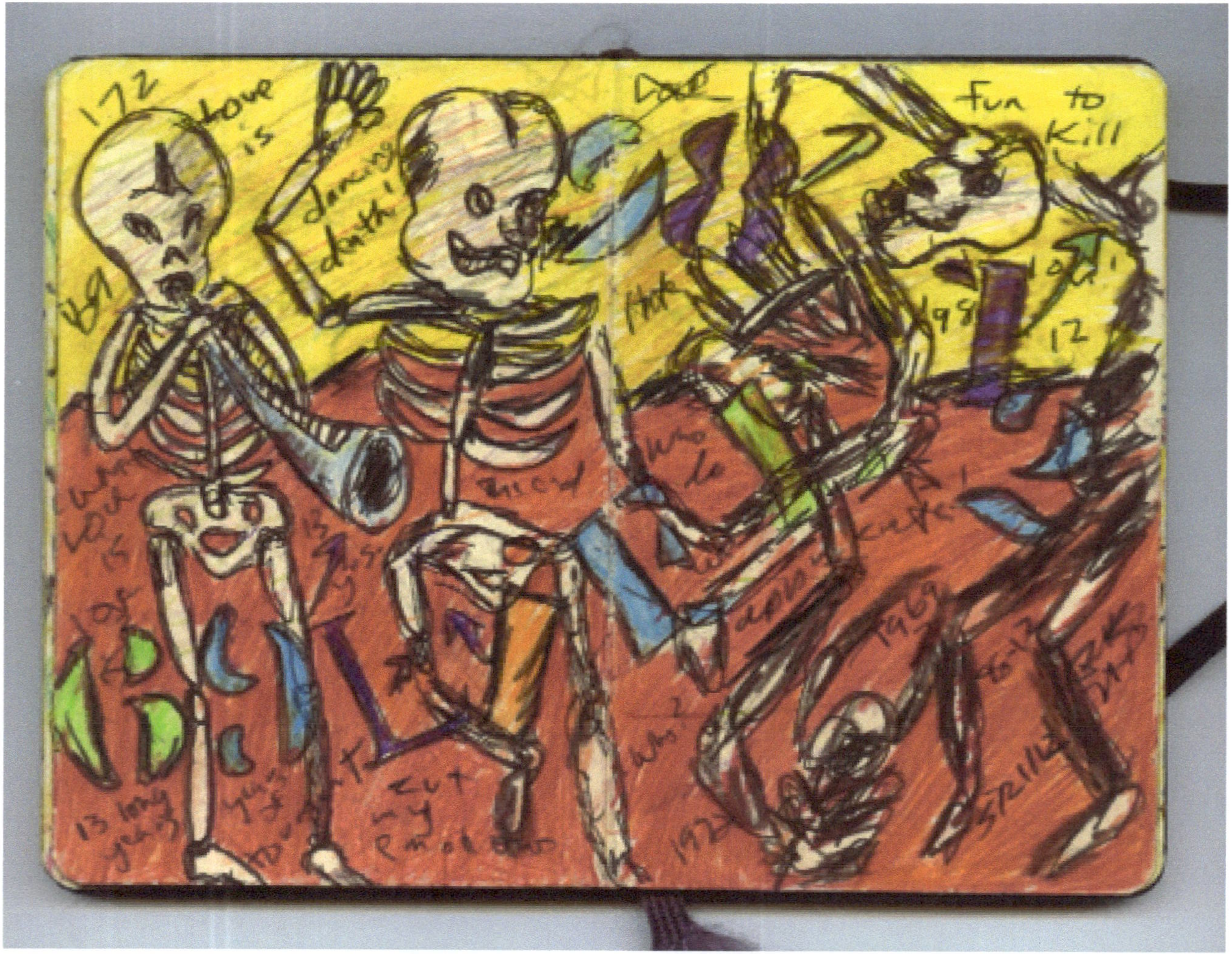

172
Love is
dancing death!
Fun to Kill
12

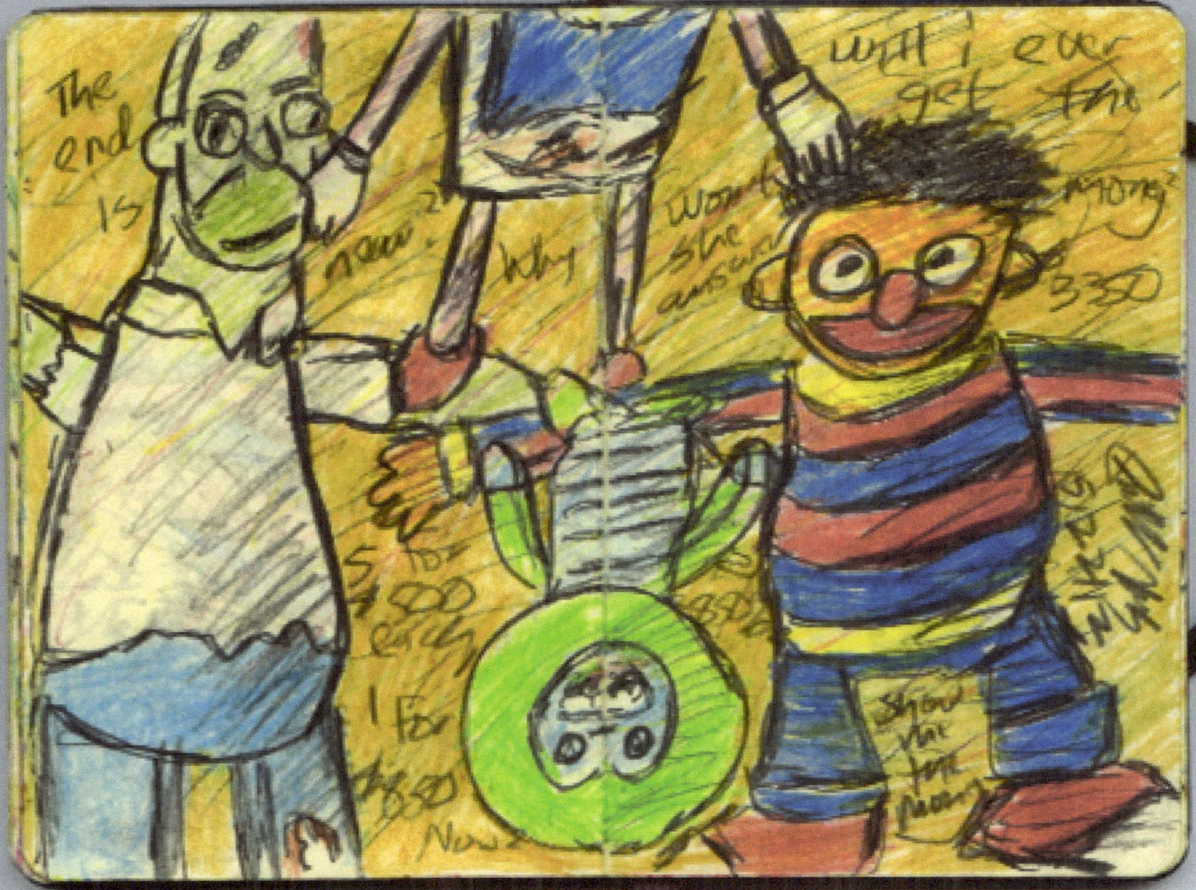
The end is now?
Why
Will I ever get the

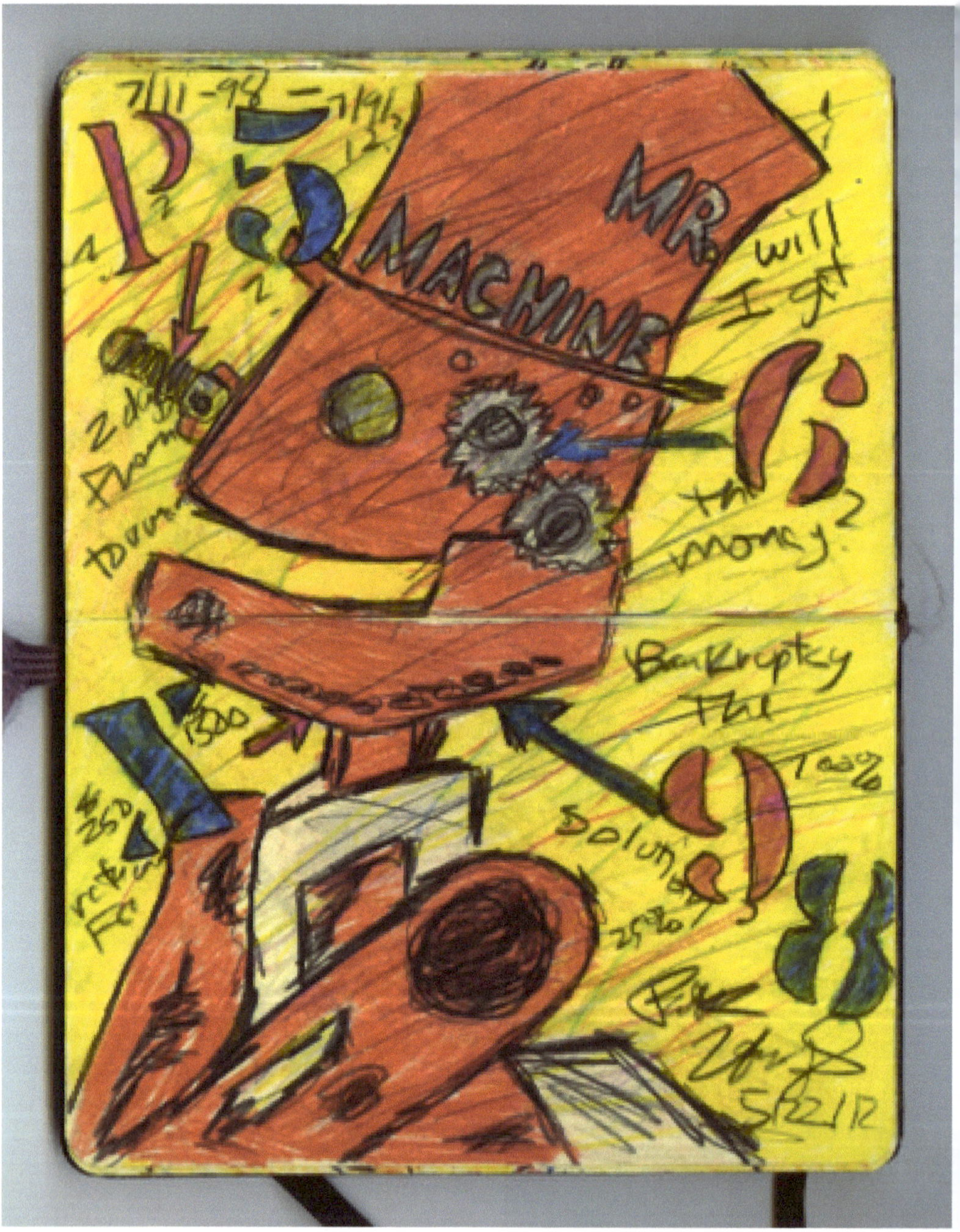
MR.
MACHINE
will
money.
Bankruptcy
5/22/12

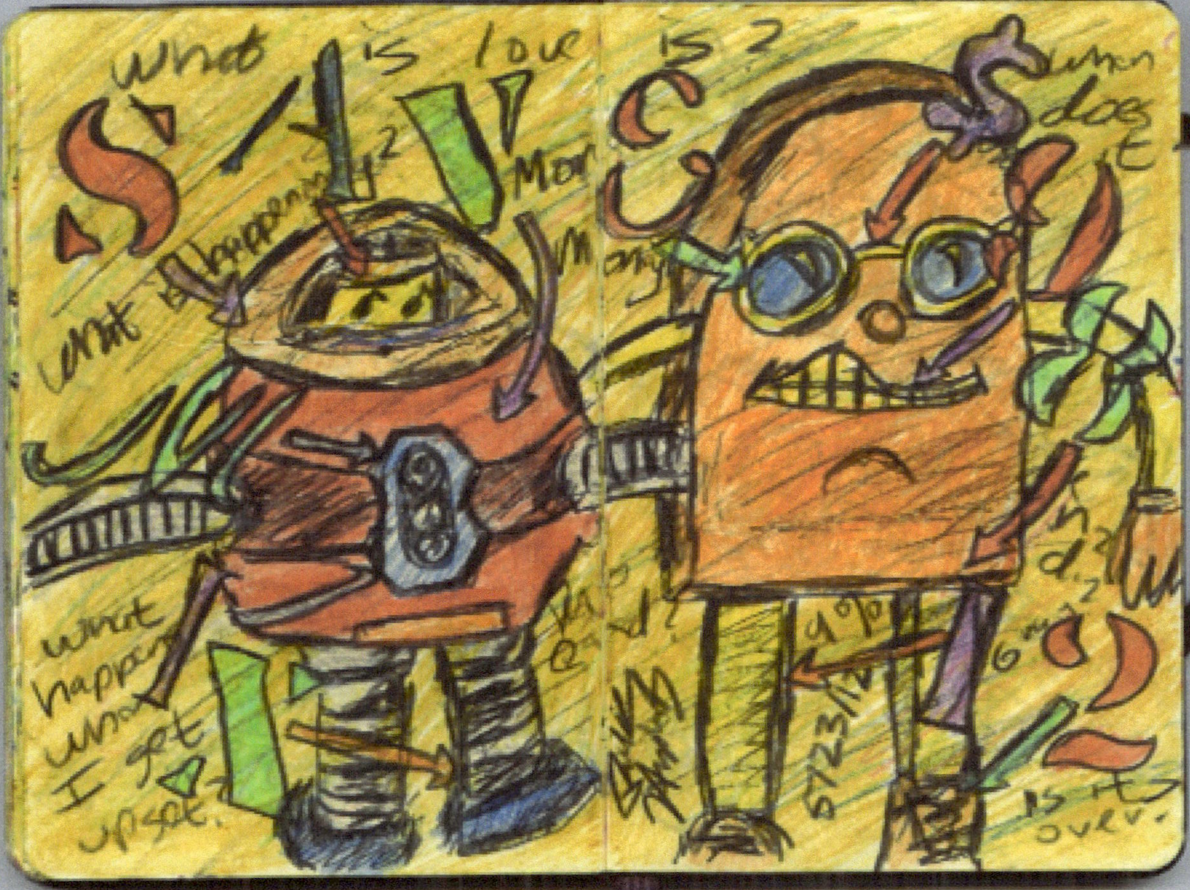
What is love is ?
What is happening ?
What happens when I get upset.
when does it end ?
is it over.

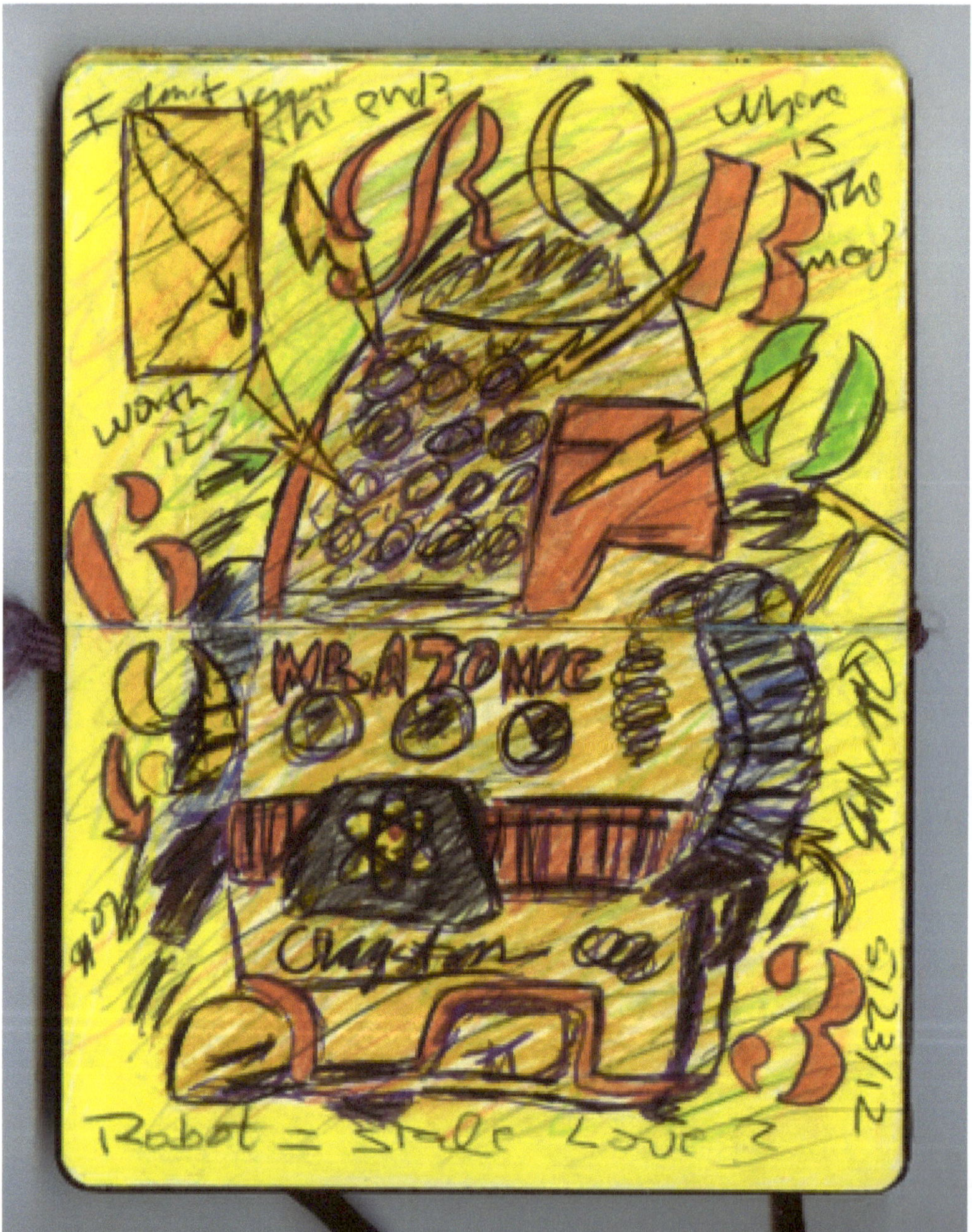
worth it?
MR. ATOMIC
Robot = Stale Love 3
5/23/12

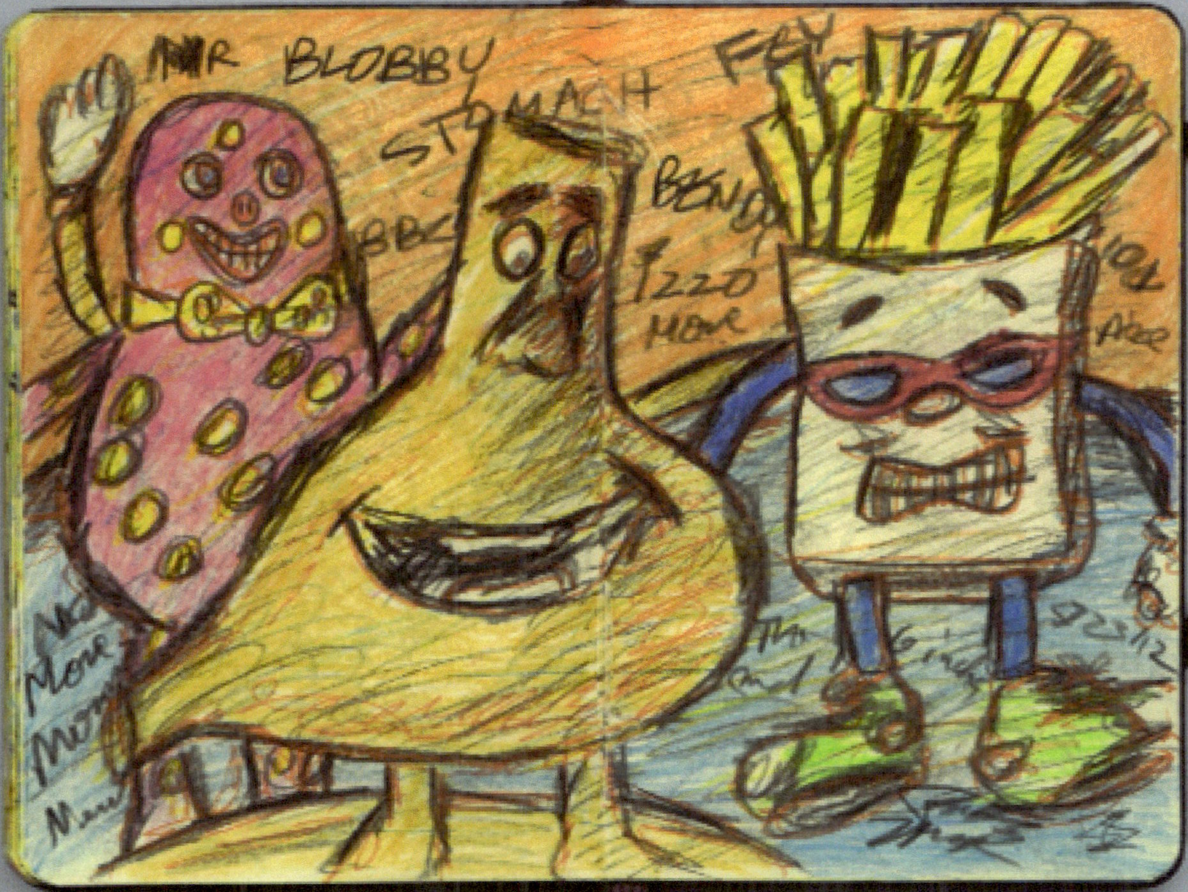
MR BLOBBY
STOMACH
FRY

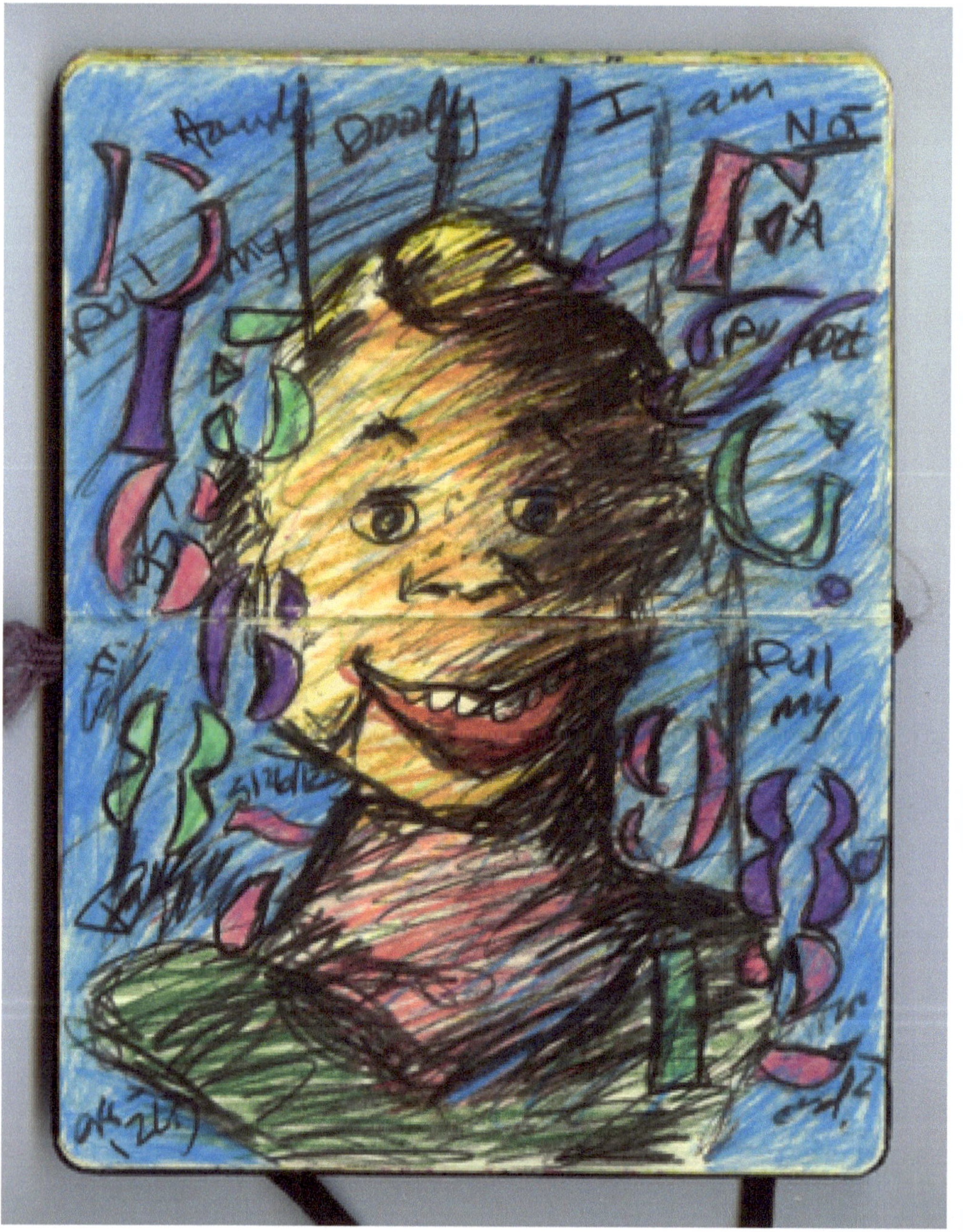
I am NOT
pull my

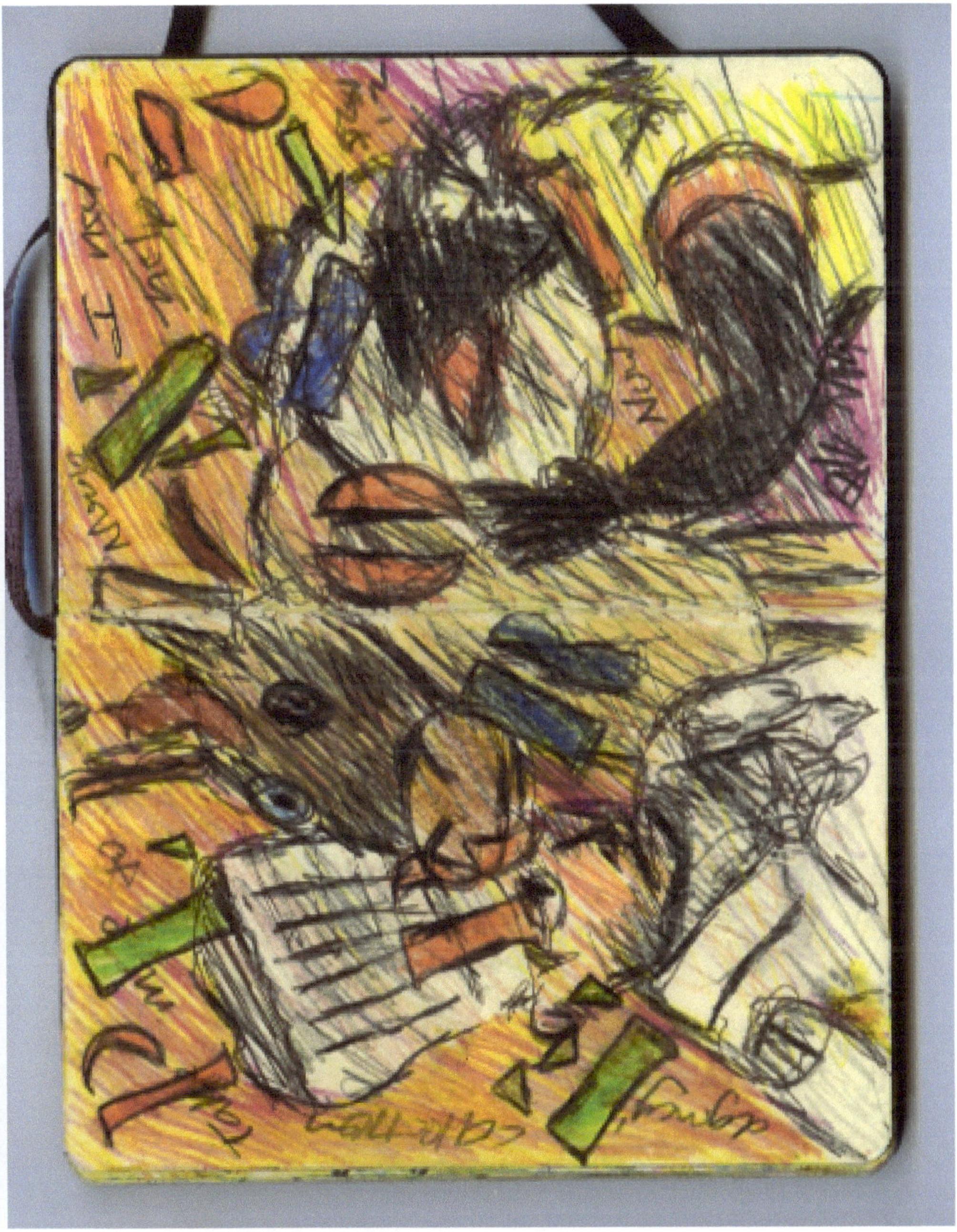

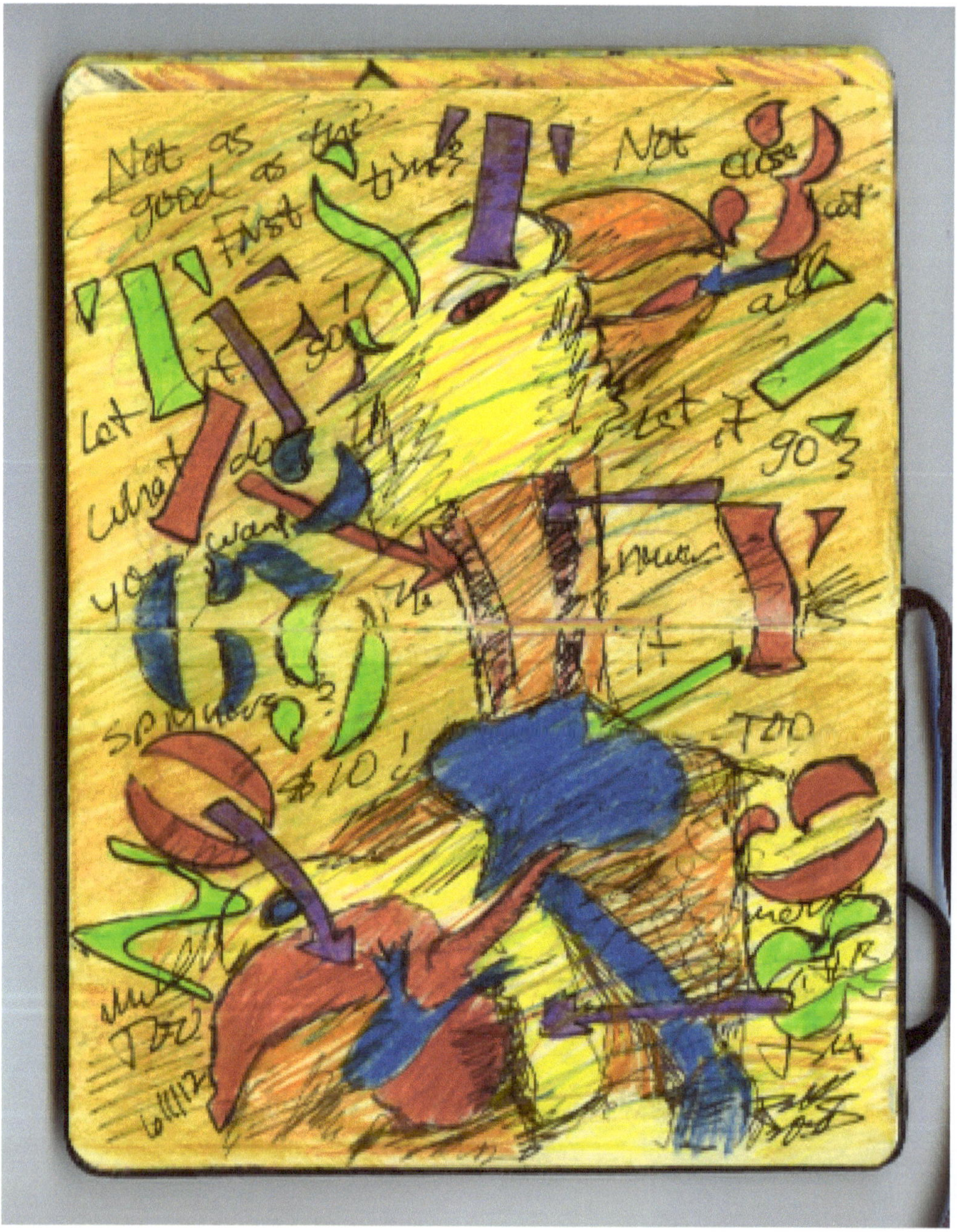
Not as good as the First time!
Not close
Let it
Let it go
what do you want
Too
$10!

www.ingramcontent.com/pod-product-compliance
Lightning Source LLC
Chambersburg PA
CBHW041143180526
45159CB00002BB/713
* 9 7 8 1 4 8 4 0 3 0 2 5 7 *